THE ANATOMY OF MELODY

EXPLORING THE SINGLE LINE OF SONG

THE ANATOMY OF MELODY
EXPLORING THE SINGLE LINE OF SONG

ALICE PARKER

GIA Publications, Inc.
Chicago

The Anatomy of Melody
Exploring the Single Line of Song

Alice Parker

Cover design and layout: Martha Chlipala
Music engraving: Paul Burrucker
Copy editor: Elizabeth Bentley

G-6765
ISBN-13: 978-1-62277-344-2

GIA Publications, Inc.
7404 South Mason Avenue, Chicago 60638
www.giamusic.com
Copyright © 2006 GIA Publications, Inc.

CONTENTS

THE EXPLOSIVE COMBINATION: MELODY

MELODIC STYLES

THE NEW ELEMENT

EAR PLAY AND EYE PLAY

NOTATION: THE BAR SINISTER

COMMUNICATING THE SONG

FIGURES

FOREWORD—LIFE WITHOUT MELODY

W E ARE LIVING in a culture that doesn't value melody, one that seems to have lost touch with this primal means of expression. We are surrounded by sounds so insistent, so varied in intent and clangor, that we've forgotten how to listen to a single line. In fact, we don't really listen to each other speak anymore because there are too many distractions luring us away from the unadorned human voice. We've lost the basic, easy connection between speech and song that makes speech musical and song communicative. We're perilously close to losing silence: in the electronic world, silence means disconnection.

There's no escaping the fact that we live in a visually oriented world. Pictures, symbols, and transitory images surround us, moving so quickly that we can't keep up with them. (Have we also forgotten how to look?) The eye has primacy; the ear is neglected.

Through the media's constant barrage, we are subjected to endless chatter, listening to tunes written in an unceasing quest for momentary fame and ingesting surface information that rarely delves below the surface. We are being deprived, through overload, of our principal senses.

Individual participation is the key to reawakening. What kind of music can we make that will connect us to the world of tone and time, to the vast palette of emotional colors this world can open to us? Our own lone human voice begins the identification with the delights of sound. It is the bedrock onto which other musical structures can be erected. If we have not heard a parent sing for joy or have not sung to our own children, this world remains other, a language to be learned rather than inherited from birth. And this is very much the state of music education in our schools today. Our children know only the songs learned from the media, those designed to be popular, but which are evanescent as the wind. Where are the songs that unite all ages in our cultural heritage? Where are the songs that don't depend on orchestration, amplification, and salesmanship to get us to listen (and, rarely, to join in)?

How did we get into this fix? If I look at the history of music in the Western world, the lessening of the influence of melody seems to occur in balance with the rise of printed music. In fact, the rise of harmony coincides with the invention of the printing press. The written symbols stop the music, allowing the writer or reader to look backward as well as forward and to create a "grammar" of chord progressions. Before this time, harmony was incidental—the vertical result of crossing melodic lines. Developing from 1600 until the present, harmony and post-harmonic systems have taken the lead. Melody is subservient, its principal function seeming to be as a basis for harmony. When harmony dominates, true melody cannot flourish.

In tandem with the page, melody tends to lose its voice—the individual singing that brings it to life. The attempt to notate the sound of one singer is futile: there are not enough markings in the articulation vocabulary to begin to describe actual sound. It's like describing an oil painting to someone blind from birth. The page can get the husk of the tune, but not the kernel—and it is totally possible to mistake disastrously the original intent of the page.

Think of the difference between a singer who works by ear and one whose allegiance is to the page. The first is born musical; the other must learn to hear pitches, to tune and count and pronounce and even to breathe. The two make very different mistakes—but the intuitive singer inhabits the world of sound, and very few page-students do. In fact, the latter have so many intellectual barriers erected that it can take years of study to break through them. (It happened to me.)

Rhythm, pitch, and text combine in vocal and instrumental melodies all over the world. The results are just as different as our spoken languages, those sounds that penetrate our ears as we develop and which we learn, miraculously, to utter with our mouths. The ability to sing is a principal function of the ear-voice-brain continuum. No one has to teach us to sing—listen to a bunch of two-year-olds. We learn specific songs, yes, or techniques of singing, but not the basic process.

Western music is the only society to list harmony right up there in the trinity of musical greats. But I don't think it belongs there. If melody (tones) and rhythm (time) are intrinsic to human beings, then harmony is a subset of melody. It is no more on the same level as melody than vertical combinations of rhythmic figures would be equal to rhythm itself. Should we say melody, harmony, rhythm, and polyrhythms? Harmony and polyrhythm are subsets because they arise out of the genre. They do not replace it.

We glory in our Western tradition of great classical music—and it is to be revered. But it is the output of one culture's thinking, and in the long view is no more important than other highly sophisticated kinds of music-making that do not depend either on the page or on harmony. (See Chinese, African, or Indonesian music.) The whole heritage of folk song is not inferior to the world of Bach, Beethoven, and Brahms; it is simply another kind of outpouring (and a far more geographically widespread one) of the human response to the world of sound.

And folk music is melody-based. Small children can sing a melody as purely as seasoned performers, and it becomes part of their psyches in ways to which orchestral literature can only aspire. When we sing the song ourselves, shaping the tones and rhythms and words into an expressive whole, it becomes part of our long-term memories, available for joy and solace throughout our lives. I remember melodies from each decade of my life, recalling the people who sang them to me and where and when I learned them. And, certainly, when I remember the great orchestral literature it is the melodies, clad in their instrumental splendor, which first come into my mind. On them hang all the textures, the rich harmonies and surprising progressions, the brilliant orchestrations and complex structures. They are the way into the appreciation of this music.

When we move to a post-melodic world, most of this is lost. When a melody is constructed out of twelve different but equal tones, it doesn't obey natural laws of structure and inevitability. (Can you sing a twelve-tone song?) When a melody is constructed to sit on top of a predetermined chord sequence, the same result is obtained. There *are* rules of melody—rules that follow natural laws of form and motion. The great songwriters are all consciously or unconsciously aware of these laws and give us melodies that live beyond their makers' life spans.

Melody ruled in Western music until the end of the nineteenth century. The great Romantic composers, Brahms, Tchaikovsky, Verdi, et al., poured forth great tunes. But when the extensions of harmonic theory seemed to be exhausted, the whole system was deemed to be dead. Tonal harmony was over, I was told in college—so a new language was needed. That is a self-fulfilling prophecy for the believer—and we've lived to see the results. We can't rationally invent a language that will supplant one that has developed over slow centuries. The natural process always wins.

So here we are at the beginning of the twenty-first century, trying to figure out how to fix what has gone wrong. Our orchestras and opera companies are struggling to rebuild their connection to the common man. Our academic and electronic composers are trying to create new languages (or recreate old ones)—but to whom are they communicating? Here is the popular music world, bereft of the great melodists of the first half of the twentieth century, trying to make do with rap, or with the kind of hard rock that limits itself to three pitches, three chords, texts without grace, and electronic volume. These appeals to physicality and emotion are in perfect balance with the over-intellectualization of the "serious" musicians. What's missing? The center—melody, pure and simple, growing out of the impulse to communicate with each other through word, time, and tone.

We regain our way by learning to listen quietly, then to mimic and to echo, as children learn to speak. We hear the difference between one voice and another, between different speech rhythms, and the ways melodic lines imprint our memories. We copy, and right away we improvise. We play the game of sounds, *ludus tonalis*. We hear and sing pitches and rhythms that are un-notatable. We learn to value songs that have lasted and discover how to sing and play with them ourselves. We can discern the difference between the tune and the setting.

All we need are ears and voice—no expensive paraphernalia, no extended study. (That can come later.) Memory and the will to communicate take over. For this is a societal process: we sing individually, but the collective sound of a singing group is one of the great life-affirming experiences open to us human beings. When our ears and voices connect in song, this makes possible a transcendental moment that releases us from our human limitations. Our society is wounded by its absence. Let's find a way to have melody again. Let's sing.

PREFACE

W<small>E ARE INQUIRING</small> into the nature of song, that which happens in our human throats when we sing without accompaniment of any kind. What is the nature of this language? Does it have a vocabulary, grammar, and identifying characteristics? Does it transmit meaning?

In almost every case, song is made up of three elements: text (words, lyrics, poems, hymns), rhythm (all the time elements of music), and pitch (all the spatial elements of music). Songs convey one kind of meaning through their words, but communicate at another level entirely through the music. Is it possible to define this second language, which seems to be beyond words? We can certainly be aware of its effect through the different ways it kindles physical and emotional responses.

This book is founded upon a love for language in all its subtle variations, both the spoken language we use every day and the musical language that so mysteriously enlarges it. It is also founded on the belief that words and music are primarily sounded and that any transfer to the page is lamentably partial. We can write only the barest bones of pitch and rhythm, articulation and style. The untutored reader cannot possibly derive an idiomatic performance from the page alone, but can sing wonderfully from the heart when the song is learned by ear. The page teaches similarity (it reduces, mechanizes), and the ear teaches variation (it enlarges, humanizes).

Fifty years of composing, conducting, coaching, and teaching have led me full circle back to ear-and-voice as the true transmitter of sound knowledge. The page is useful only when its symbols evoke living sound in the imagination of the reader. We tend to teach reading much too early in the learning process: this book is a plea for returning to beginnings. Can we hear and really concentrate on a single line of song coming from a human throat, absorbing all the feelings and personality it transmits, as well as its musical values? Can we mimic it, echo it, or even answer it with a corresponding phrase of our own? Can we dwell long enough in the single line so that the answer, the response, feels like a welcome new blossom on an old stem?

These brief chapters attempt to recreate that process— to disengage us for the moment from harmony and counterpoint, from theory and the page, and bring us back to that first delighted, instinctive response to melody we see in little children.

A Cautionary Note

Look at the page you are holding: two-dimensional, white, and covered with black squiggles. Silent. Remember what it looked like before you could read, with the calligraphy meaningful only to educated eyes. Until we add the voice to the page, it is literally mute. Here is the central paradox of writing about music. Unless we read music and words well enough to supply an appropriate sound for each symbol, those symbols are collectively meaningless. They convey some information, but no context. My belief is that a page of music conveys about 5 percent of the information needed to perform it.

A play's script is exactly analogous to an orchestral score. It suggests far more than it delivers, and it doesn't come to life until it is made sound and sight and tension and emotion through human beings. It can be read with a terrifying literalness, or it can suggest—through what is un-notatable—a new universe.

Also true of both drama and music is this: there is no such thing as a perfect reading. In both cases, the page is a recipe for performance, and each performance is unique. The voice is added through individual performers, and each actor is, *ipso facto*, original. The pages sit there, inviting us to see what we can make of them, a proposition that is endlessly enticing, yet never fully achieved.

I have come to realize over the years that a healthy mistrust of written music is the only proper starting point. The page doesn't mean what it seems. It's only a beginning (sight) not an ending (sound). Keep these thoughts in mind as you turn these pages. Does a song you know leap out at you with the immediacy of a remembered voice? Or do the symbols lie obstinately flat on the page with the attendant words similarly meaningless? To understand what I am attempting here, realize that I am trying to balance two antithetical worlds at once—those of eye and ear—and in this case, ear must always triumph not only in the notes, but in the written text where a living voice must be sounding for you to begin to respond in kind. And respond, aloud, you must! Sing, argue, affirm, correct—the page does not live until you enter into its dialogue with your ear, voice, and mind.

OVERVIEW

CHAPTER 1:
THE POWER OF MELODY

SONG COMES FROM a throat, lungs, a heart, a memory. It is primary human communication, outside the boundaries of rational thought, exploring the world of emotions through mental constructions that tend to be intuitive. The gift of writing memorable songs is rare—Schubert, Gershwin, and that great genius Anonymous had it—and seems to be based on the same forces that govern the shapes of water, of clouds, of mountain ranges. We begin with the physics of sound and end with apotheosis…energy, pure.

I have spent most of my life working with melodies, singing continuously as a child and in formal and informal groups as I grew older, concentrating in organ and composition in college, and then majoring in choral conducting at Juilliard with Robert Shaw, which gave my life its direction. In working with him, I felt as though I'd never really listened before, never been aware of the subtleties of living sound, of the incredible variety of sounds the throat can produce. We began working together on arrangements for albums recorded by the Shaw Chorale, and I spent hours, days, and weeks in the New York Public Library sifting through thousands of songbooks. I began to get a sense of what melodies would work for me, for us, which would produce a wonderful arrangement or which would lead to okay but uninspiring results.

The answer was always within the single line itself—not the setting, the harmonies (actual or implied), or any of its elements separately. The tune itself (text + rhythm + pitch) contained, like a seed, all the elements needed for its growth. If something was missing, one might try to replace it with cleverness, but never with profundity. Over the twenty years Robert Shaw and I worked together, I came to have a profound respect for any melody that lasted, any melody that successive generations have sung and loved and kept in their hearts and passed on to the next.

Let us look at one folk song (Figure 1.1), trying to identify the elements within it that combine to give it this enduring and endearing structure. Consider first the whole song, for as children we learn songs by wholes, by hearing them lovingly sung and then joining in with bits and snatches until the whole is securely lodged in memory. From hearing we get the tone of voice, the unique personality of the singer, subtle articulations, the storytelling, mood-setting, and immediate communication. We are not aware of notes and rhythms or breathing and tone production, but of arching phrases, motion and climax, bodily involvement, and the invitation to join in. None of this can be notated.

FIGURE 1.1. "Oh, Shenandoah"

Text and tune: Early American

More verses:

> Oh, Shenandoah, I love your daughter;
> Way hay, you rolling river,
> Oh, Shenandoah, I love your daughter.
> Way hay, we're bound away, 'cross the wide Missouri.
>
> Oh, Shenandoah, I'm bound to leave you;
> Way hay, you rolling river,
> Oh, Shenandoah, I'll not deceive you.
> Way hay, we're bound away, 'cross the wide Missouri.

"Oh, Shenandoah" evokes longing, memories of home, the curves of water, and the surging of waves. It is not a work song. The rhythm is not that of repeated, regular muscular exertion, but of the slow swell of the ocean. The curves of the melody itself are released only when sung freely, when the voice can expand on the high notes and move with infinite flexibility through gentle rises and falls. It is a fo'castle shanty, sung at night in the sailors' quarters when the work is done, keeping the rhythms of the sea on an inland river.

The text is ambiguous and often varied (as it is in many folk songs). The title may refer to an Indian chief, a river, or the region around it. The refrains built into the piece ("Way hay, you rolling river" and "Way hay, we're bound away, 'cross the wide Missouri") suggest work or geography, but the verses are about love. "Oh, Shenandoah, I long to hear you" could refer to all three, and the third, love, could be a long-ago or a very present desire. Dialogue is built into the song: the solo voice begins, and the listeners respond.

FIGURE 1.2. "Oh, Shenandoah"—melodic curves

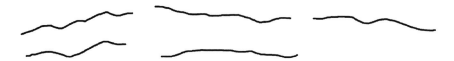

If we trace the mountain-range curves of the phrases, they look like birds soaring up, then slowly descending (Figure 1.2). The five phrases are perfectly balanced within: rise and fall, tension and release, final consummation.

The written rhythms betray the ambiguity of beat. They move back and forth between 4/4 and 3/4, from call to response, without haste. This is the rhythm of thoughtful speech, with the pauses that memory or emotion supply. What is this freedom of beat? It is not license to do whatever one wants, for there are inner compulsions. The solo lines tell the story. They can be conversational, idiomatically sounded. The refrains need more "beat" just to keep the singers together. Think of the rhythm within the text phrases "rolling river," "bound away," and "Missouri." (Say that last word aloud. How do you phrase it? Can you sustain the first or last syllable? Accent either one? Can you sing it the way you say it?)

Igor Stravinsky writes in the *Dialogues and a Diary* by Stravinsky and Robert Craft: "To me, the relation of tempo and meaning is a primary question of musical order, and until I am certain that I have found the right tempo, I cannot compose." If tempo stands for the time elements of music, then it seems strange to me that he makes no reference to the pitch elements. I need to add "and sonority" before his final three words. Tempo and sonority seem to be the underlying generative forces that define the two universes in which music exists: rhythm and pitch, time and space. For "Oh, Shenandoah" the tempo should be unhurried with inner flexibility and contrast; sonority is deep—the depth of the river, the ocean, rich and full. Both elements echo the watery motion built into the song itself.

I still have not mentioned the key or specific pitches and durations. The notes and rhythms that we sing, those remaining in our memories, are like the froth at the top of the curling wave, the inevitable result of forces below and above them: gravity, tide, wind. Great songs have this connection between the depths of communicative power and the tiny building blocks of their construction. When we hear a superb performance, both of these elements work together in a powerful evocation of mood and place. In folk songs, the specific pitches and rhythms are always open to change. As a consequence, they suffer from being written down, from being constrained by the definiteness of the page. We can follow the page's signals exactly and totally miss the song. The page makes it look as though the song were instantly retrievable: "Follow me," it says, "and you get it, always and reliably the same." The human transmission of song is the opposite: the personal language of the singer, inviting you to find the song in your own voice and experience. Does the singer lead you into the song? Convince you to enter into its world? Evoke a place, a time, and a person? If not, the song is not present, only its shell.

I sometimes think of song as an invisible presence always around us, an ever-present possibility hovering like a cloud above us. The song is implicit until it is sounded—then it begins to pulse and glow, come to life, flourish, and fade away. The first sound released into the room either conjures forth the melody or makes it impossible for it to live. The first sound followed by others that never break the chain creates a structure as sturdy—and as fleeting—as a tree, a leaf, or a flower and as flowing as water.

In the end, the real questions about the song are: Can you sing it so that the song is both true to itself and gives you pleasure? So that it holds the attention of a listener? So that it invites us to join in? I can see myself in my kitchen, singing to myself as I do dishes; then the communication is between the song and my voice. Then imagine that a three-year-old girl enters. If I sing to her, I'm enlarging the circle, singing it differently, moving the focus to her using my whole body to communicate. The final step is getting her to join in, singing in a way that invites her participation. Singing less, inviting more, giving her the song. That is when the circle grows, when the song is passed along. That is when music is most present, when it captures us in its spell, when it transforms us by its presence. Anything less is not enough.

— REFLECTIONS —

- Chant "Oh, Shenandoah"
- How much freedom from meter is there?
- Try reading the song in strict rhythms and then freely. What is the difference? Which do you prefer?
- Which notes can be held longer? Where can you hurry? How are you breathing?
- Can you hear "Oh, Shenandoah" sung by a man? A woman? A child? A big voice? A light voice? An opera singer? What is the difference? Which do you prefer?
- Sing it for yourself alone.
- Now, pretend there is one other person. Can you coax a child to join in?
- Now you are with a group of friends, inviting them to join in. How do you feel? How would your singing change with a group of strangers? With a paying audience? Which do you prefer?
- How would you lead the song in each instance above? What kind of motions would you use?
- Can you write down the song so that it looks like what you are singing? Make up your own notation. (It's to remind you, not for someone else.)
- Do you know other songs that can be sung this freely? Try "Sometimes I Feel Like a Motherless Child" (Figure1.3).

FIGURE 1.3. "Sometimes I Feel Like a Motherless Child"

Text and tune: American spiritual

More verses:

Sometimes I feel like I gotta no home. (3x)
A long way from home. (2x)

Sometimes I feel like I'm almost gone. (3x)
A long way from home. (2x)

Remember that if you take extra time to breathe or just hold a colorful syllable longer than notated, you're beginning the path to speech rhythms. Where will this work?

— DAUGHTER OF THE MUSES —

She first appeared to me years ago, looking like the cover of a nineteenth-century parlor song: young with unbound hair, leaning on a windowsill, looking out with a dreamy gaze—engraved, formal, proper. Her flowing gown was reminiscent of the muses, but she was a bit too ethereal to carry much weight.

A later, more helpful apparition seemed to be a close relative of the good witch Glinda in *The Wizard of Oz*. Remember how she floated over the hills in a magic bubble that faded away as it landed, revealing the glowing presence within? She was—is—"Lady Music," a magic presence indeed who inhabits the upper air, materializing wherever true music is being made. She doesn't come if there's talk about music or if unmusical sounds are being made or if the music-making is perfunctory or dull. She lingers in the shadows until a clear, true phrase rings out, compelling the listener to hear and to become involved, until both are lost in the music. Then she slowly gains shape and form, becoming more and more radiant as phrase follows phrase, building arches of sound. She fades away as the sound waves die in the silence that follows such art. As Shakespeare wrote of Orpheus in *Henry VIII*:

> Everything that heard him play,
> Even the billows of the sea,
> Hung their heads, and then lay by.
> In sweet music is such art,
> Killing care and grief of heart
> Fall asleep, or hearing, die.

The truth is, we never can see her. We can't ask her to appear, or to wait until we've finished rehearsing this phrase, or even know when she is fully present. The moment we remove ourselves enough from the music-making to look for her—she's gone. We, too, as conductors or teachers or performers or listeners, are part of the whole experience, and it's the whole that she represents.

Fanciful? Oh, yes—but useful precisely as a measure for what we are doing in rehearsals, concerts, services, classrooms, or studios. The question is: For how much of the time are we making meaningful sound? Are we woodshedding the notes? Telling stories? Teaching theory? Allowing unmusical sounds to be made and then scolding the makers?

She scorns all such endeavors because unmusical sounds are un-music. Any time we sing or play without attention, she is un-present. Yet she can be there as a family sings around the dinner table or in the elementary school classroom or the choir rehearsal or the exalted performance. She follows the physical laws of pitch and rhythm, of musical energy and expressivity, of the language of the heart. She is never fooled. She is always ready to appear. Are we ready for her? Do we invite her presence? How often?

CHAPTER 2:
SONG AS POSSIBILITY

THE FOLLOWING BITTERSWEET love song from the British Isles sets up a rueful counterpoint between what we know and what we don't know, between certainty of key and mood and the undermining of both in the last line. Different singers interpret it in varied ways. I love to hear it without accompaniment, sung rather freely.

FIGURE 2.1. "I Know Where I'm Going"

I know where I'm go-in'____ and I know who's goin' with me.

I know who I love,____ but the dear knows who I'll mar-ry.

Text and tune: British Isles

What do we need to make music? Breath and voice, confidence, something to sing about. Not a book, reading, voice lessons, theory, or poetry—not even an audience or co-singer. It's as if song is built into our subconscious beings, and all we need is to open our ears and mouths and join in. Children who have been sung to sing back, echoing, varying, and playing. Song is always waiting for release into the air around us.

What is a song? Is it what's written on the page? No, because there is no sound there, only a diagram for sound. Is it in one particular person's singing? Yes, but that's only one possibility of many. Is it something we learned as a child? Well, yes, but again song in the memory, or in the imagination, lacks sound—vibrating columns of air—and is thus theoretical rather than real.

My answer is that any song is like a seed of possibilities that waits for a human throat to bring it to life. Not only does each voice sing it differently, but it's impossible for even the same singer to sing it twice exactly the same way because the variables are so numerous and the shadings so subtle. This re-embodiment of song is a natural, dynamic process following nature's law of endless, subtle variation. The song becomes incarnate for only the time that the sound lasts. Our technology really leads us astray on this point. We can play a recording over and over and get the same performance each time, but this is not true in the concert hall. The written score looks as though it would lead to the same result each time, but, in fact, it is always different. The same conductor changes over time; the same orchestra sounds different under different conductors; the centuries, countries, and halls are never the same. Thus it is with the simple song in different throats.

I remember attending a recital of first-year vocal students in which each song was carefully prepared, but the singers were so conscious of proper tone production, of being correct to teacher and page, that little music seeped through. What is the difference when we hear a masterful singer? How can we penetrate to the core of the song? Pitches and rhythms are only the building blocks of music; technique, like the page or concert etiquette, is the means to an end, not an end in itself. Range, tessitura, timbre, form, tempo, beat, etc., vary from one song to another and from one performance to another. But what is the irreducible whole? What does the song communicate?

Mood seems to come first of all. If we had a template for each human emotion (how many are there?) and then began mixing these into the combinations we live with every day (how often do we have unalloyed joy or sorrow?) we could measure how songs become soundings for our emotional depths. Here are releases from pressure, conveyors of comfort, joy, or sorrow, acceptable expressions of murderous rage or lust or despair. (This is not by any means "mood music," "music to do something else by," or "music not to listen to.")

These moods are expressed through energy, the physical laws of motion as sounded in pitches and rhythms. How do we get something to begin moving? I remember an eye-catching demonstration by my high school physics teacher involving a heavy stack of books placed on a single sheet of paper. He stated that the books had to "catch on" that you wanted them to move—if you didn't make it clear, they wouldn't—and he swiftly pulled the paper from underneath them. "But if you work with them gently," he continued, "they come along." And so they did, obediently following the slow, steady tug on the paper. It's easy to keep anything going once it is started, and then you have to apply the same reasoning to get it to stop—either the calamitous slamming on of brakes or the controlled gradual slowing.

I'm amazed at how few people think of music in this way. Where do we find examples of this kind of energy? We find it in the movements of water, for one: the rippling around stones (the Zen path of least resistance); the increasing turbulence of approaching storm, the gathering and ebbing wave on the beach. Where does the motion begin, gather energy, crest, climax, release energy, slow, and stop? I have asked untutored listeners to tell me whether the music we are listening to is increasing tension or releasing it. They answer correctly each time. Yet the music student is often completely unaware that this is the underlying force of those notes on the page, that without this physical knowledge the notes are only empty symbols.

— REFLECTIONS —

Finding the voice—"I Know Where I'm Going" (Figure 2.1):

- Become the singer, as though you were in a play. What has just happened to make you have to sing?

- What are you feeling? Sad? Angry? Resigned? Loving? Indifferent?

- What changes with different emotions? Describe each tone of voice. Which feels best to you now?

- What kind of voice suits the song? Light/heavy? High/low? Young/old?

- What solo instrument would suit it best? String? Wind? Brass?

- Try different tempos: slow, medium, fast.

- Move in strict rhythm, as notated. Try the song partly free: where can you hold back? Try the song very free: does this work?

- What is the form of the song? Is there any repetition?

- Where is the climax? The resolution? Do you feel "at home" at the end? Is the song over? Should it be?

- Try singing it as if you were alone and remembering; singing to a lover, teasing; with a friend, confiding; or with a disapproving adult, defiant.

- Sing all four verses. What is the emotional movement through the song? Can you characterize each verse? Where is the climax of the whole song? How do you get to it? Leave it? Can you imagine repeating the first verse at the end, remembering?

More verses ("I Know Where I'm Going"—p. 13):

I have stockings of silk,
And shoes of fine green leather;
Combs to buckle my hair,
And a ring for every finger.

Some say he's black.
But I say he's bonny:
Fairest of them all
Is my handsome, winsome Johnny.

Feather beds are soft,
And painted rooms are bonny,
But I would leave them all
To go with my love, Johnny.

BUILDING BLOCKS

CHAPTER 3:
IN THE BEGINNING IS THE WORD

THIS SIMPLE MELODY is a spinning song with slow-moving phrases that cast an incantatory spell. The place names are from a mythical Irish past, implanted into memory by a long-ago love.

FIGURE 3.1. "In Balinderry"

Text and tune: Irish traditional

Words are not just squeezed under a line of notes to make a sung melody. It's actually quite the other way: the melody (notes and rhythms) reflects the words and depends on their precise idiomatic pronunciation, not just their meaning.

Consider the complexity of the act of speech, how our vocal cords, lips, teeth, tongue, and resonating cavities move with each consonant and vowel. This instrument is constantly changing shape as it produces sound, and that's only part of it. The other great part is the aspect of time, the speed at which we speak (constantly changing) and the incredibly subtle ways in which words are grouped into phrases, pauses, and curves of rapid patter, each separated by breath and contrasted with silence. Listen to a baby in its early cooings. The baby is imitating the rise and fall of the mother's voice and later on perhaps whole sentences of babble. Here are all the qualities of language except specific words and sense. That's the musical part of speech.

Now think of your first attempts at learning another language, how laboriously you memorized the vocabulary and grammar, and how stubbornly the speech refused to flow, that easy trick young children master without conscious effort. A case in point is the beginning-to-be ubiquitous use of electronic voices telling us to "Watch your step" or "The door is a-jar." While electronic voices have undoubtedly improved in their quality, it has taken fifty years of work to get this far—and I still would not care to hear one read a poem!

A musical friend was quick to grasp the possibilities of the tape recorder when it came on the market. As a choral conductor and scholar of sound, he decided to record the separate vocalizations of each vowel and consonant in a simple phrase like "Hello, how are you?" and then snip and fit them together to make the spoken sound. After hours of work, he gave up. Changing one part changed all the others, and he never could get the phrase to flow.

22

All this is to say that we perform a marvelously complex activity when we speak, however crudely. The ear remembers the sounds it has heard from infancy and gives them back through the vocal cords. The tiny child forms without difficulty the vowels (e.g., the French "u") and consonants (e.g., the German "ch") he or she has imprinted on the mind, and, indeed, cannot later learn to pronounce them as well. Babies are born with ears and voice boxes and the innate ability to mimic the language sounds around them, the music in the words. Only later do they learn to speak, to put words and grammar together into complex ideas. And, of course, it is this preliterate flow of language that concerns me here.

I am constantly searching for texts to set. I love lyric poetry and the kind of prose that approaches poetry (the King James Bible, for instance). I can tell immediately as I read whether the melody hidden in those words will reveal itself to me. I feel the sounds in my throat as I read, and they either "sing" or do not. The lyric brevity of Emily Dickinson is music to my ears, but the expansive parabolas of sound in Walt Whitman (which I also love) are not. There's no accounting for it. We are each different and respond to different cues. (Thank goodness!)

When I start to set a poem, I begin by copying it out in longhand, noting all the punctuation, line indentations, verse separations, and spellings. Then I memorize it, repeating aloud until I know it by heart (what a wonderful phrase). Often I will then test myself by writing it out again from memory, checking that each jot and tittle is correct. I want to put myself in the mind and voice of the poet, feeling as though I myself had created these lines. As I speak, the phrase curves grow more and more familiar, and the separating pauses take on their own pattern. I'm digging down through the surface of the poem to its inmost structure—rhyme, assonance, accent and cross-accent, pause and rush forward. The text is the rhythm; the spoken sound becomes, in our inadequate notation, the sung rhythm.

Here is a poem by Emily Dickinson. It is full of her own punctuation—dashes. Do they mean expressive pauses? Can you glimpse her vision? Can you read the poem aloud in a way that transmits it to a listener?

Exultation is the going
Of an inland soul to sea,
Past the houses—past the headlands—
Into deep Eternity—

Bred as we, among the mountains,
Can the sailor understand
The divine intoxication
Of the first league out from land?
—Emily Dickinson (#76)

When I was working on my opera *The Ponder Heart*, setting a delightfully comic story by Eudora Welty, I had to find a musical "voice" for the narrator. Edna Earle, of course, has wonderful words supplied by Ms. Welty—whole paragraphs of them as she tells the tale. Could I set them in a way that kept all their southern speech flavor without distortion? I found I had to copy them onto manuscript paper under a blank staff and then literally notate the speech rhythms as I read aloud. Not surprisingly, the basic meter was 7/8 (we speak in little groups of twos and threes, not a constant 3/4 or 4/4) with fairly frequent variants. Even the rests between phrases, sentences, and paragraphs were measured before I ever added any pitches. And even these came from the text! The easy rise and fall of speech became the widened scale of song with extreme highs and lows reserved for very dramatic moments.

FIGURE 3.2. "My Uncle Daniel"

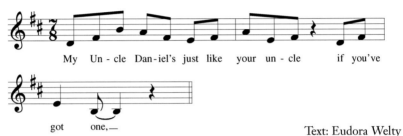

Text: Eudora Welty
Tune: Copyright © 1982 Alice Parker

Take that simple phrase, "Hello, how are you?" Imagine it set by Mozart (yes, in English). By Britten. By Stravinsky. It's always different, isn't it? No matter who is speaking or singing, in whatever dialect, the phrase changes. If we had the needles and gauges to record all the variables, could we ever say it exactly the same way twice?

Accentuation is enormously important. Listen to people around you speaking—on a bus or at the other end of the room. The rise-and-fall of the pitch may be limited in scope, but the pressure of the accent is amazingly variable. In trying to present a visual image, I think of someone bouncing on a trampoline with gauge lines painted on a wall behind. It takes great control to get a steady rhythm going, and that's not the aim in speech. Here, the basic rule is: no two adjacent sounds are ever the same. The jumper on a trampoline depresses the surface a different amount with each pass, taking longer with the deeper levels to go down and come up, moving more quickly with the shallower falls.

That amazing variability of speech has to be built into whatever language is sung. In our page-driven age, we tend to shove the word into the note value, as if the quarter note were an ice cube with the syllable frozen inside. I'd much rather think of the notation, both pitch and rhythm, as being at the service of the word or phrase as naturally spoken, with all the subtlety preserved. My inner vision is of a word, in its lumpy variability, being bathed in pitch and duration as though these were precious oils being poured over it.

If we really believed that speech underlies the song, we teachers, singers, and conductors would approach songs completely differently. We would begin with the text, lovingly read aloud and learned well in the mood and rhythms of the song. We would find the music in the text first, as though we ourselves were going to set it, then notice the specifics of what the composer had done. We would observe and act on any helpful hints in tempo indication, expression markings, fermatas—all indications for subtlety, for deviation from the prison of the page. We would know that only when the solo singer or chorus can read the text beautifully in the rhythms of the song is it time to add the pitches. *Last, not first.*

The pitches come last because, willy-nilly, pitches have duration. If we learn them before we have the rhythms of the song clearly in mind, then we learn them incorrectly and have to change. This goes a long way toward explaining much of the dull singing around us. I'm totally opposed to learning the notes and rhythms before adding the words—they can never, then, regain their primacy. Words first!

Try it now with these words. Read them aloud. Create a mood. Notice the speech rhythms, where you hesitate, and where you hurry. Think of the first "Number" as an invitation: "Let's count." Now try intoning the words, reciting them on the same pitch. (As hard as I try to preserve the spoken rhythms, something changes them as I sing.

Exactly what changes? Does it allow more or less freedom?) Now add
the pitches. Do they make it easier or harder to keep the text rhythms?

FIGURE 3.3. "By'm Bye"

Text and tune: American traditional

— REFLECTIONS —

**The speech beneath the song—"In Balinderry" (metric),
"By'm Bye" (free):**

- Read aloud the first verse of "In Balinderry" (Figure 3.1). Can you make it sound Irish? How do you do this using consonants? Vowels? Tone of voice?
- Try it Scots, British, Northern U.S., and Southern U.S. What changes?
- Read it as though:

  You were stating well-known facts.

  You were leading a guided tour.

  You had been to each island.

  You were madly in love with Phelimy Diamond.

  You were at your spinning wheel, remembering.

- Now read it in the rhythms notated.

  Can you find a comfortable tempo? (Remember the spinning.)

  Can you differentiate each island?

  Can you caress the name "Phelimy"?

- How long do you wait between verses? How does it begin? Climax? End?
- Now sing it. Can you do this without losing any of the subtlety of your speech?
- Follow the same path with "By'm Bye," (Figure 3.3) beginning with Southern speech.
- Try it metrically, then freely. How free can you be?
- How long can you wait between phrases? Which words can you lengthen? Where must you keep moving?

- Imagine you are holding a child in your arms, gazing out the window.

  Can you put the child to sleep?

  Can you teach the counting?

  Is there a climax?

- Now sing all the verses.

  Can you make each one different?

  What is the energy curve of the whole song?

More verses ("By'm Bye"—p. 27):

By'm bye, by'm bye, stars shining.
Number: number four, number five, number six.
Good Lord, by'm bye, by'm bye.

By'm bye, by'm bye, stars shining.
Number: number seven, number eight, number nine.
Good Lord, by'm bye.

- Choose two songs from this book. Write out the words as a poem, and then try reading them in the patterns suggested above. Can you notate the rhythms?

—THE LADDER OF LANGUAGE—

(start at the lowest rung and climb up)

Fulfilled Silence
all previous sounds
distilled into one
all-sound

Song without Words
abstraction; implied
meaning; what words
cannot say

Song
adding pitch

Poetry
metaphor; expanding
limits; rhyme and rhythm

Human Speech
emotions; information
(naming, needs)

Animal and Bird
increasingly melodic
and expressive

Wind and Water
natural sounds

Vibration
motion, breath

Inchoate Silence
blank emptiness

CHAPTER 4:
THE ETERNAL DANCE

ROCK AND ROLL, polka, waltz, two-step, minuet, samba, and tarantella—dances have their characteristic rhythms and beats, moods and motions. As with speech, national and cultural patterns abound: contrast the undulations of the hula with the ramrod focus of Celtic step-dancing, or the seductive languor of the tango with the elegance of the minuet. To say that they are in duple or triple meter is to state only the most obvious. What really distinguishes one from the other?

I've long pondered the success of the Bach keyboard suites: how do they overcome the sameness of six or seven movements all in one key (with a relative minor every now and then)? Those of us trained in the tonal exuberance of the nineteenth century expect far more tonal movement. We assume that harmonic variety will be the key to listener satisfaction. But something else is going on here. These suites are collections of dances, with distinctions of tempo, accent, and articulation. The defining factor, I believe, is the possibility of different motions in the human body. It is almost to say that musical rhythm equals physical movement or, conversely, that "rhythm" without a human context is dry and sterile indeed: a metronome.

The human body is confined by gravity: it is rooted to and in the floor. Much dance derives power from the attempt to overcome this limit. Consider the breathtaking leaps in ballet and Cossack folk patterns. Other dancers affirm gravity. Look at Martha Graham or

Alvin Ailey. Dance is also circumscribed by arm and torso movements as in classical Indian dance. The body may crouch low to the ground, move gently along a narrow path, and leave unexplored the wide extensions of arms and legs. Or it may do the opposite, or any combination of possible motions. Each dance is as different as each human being or each grain of sand: individual, unique. Unless we find the dance in the music, we cannot communicate its power.

Tempo and accent make up the next layer to examine. Every musician knows that getting just the right tempo is a key to successful performance, yet how do we determine the tempo of an unknown song? There's no problem if we know the dance. We move, and the movement tells us. Otherwise it's a process of trial and error, or gradually pulling the various sections together until a tempo is found that unites them all. Of course, changes in the underlying tempo are possible. Life is full of *accelerandos* and *ritardandos*. But in most folk dances, changes of tempo are anathema. (Listen to 1920s jazz; there's not one speeding or slowing, even at the end. I'm sure that one too many missed, flubbed, or insecure beats must be the origin of the phrase "Shoot the piano player"!)

Let us turn back to a single-line folksong melody.

Here is a nineteenth-century American tune, probably from Appalachia, with a modal melody and a twinkly-eyed humor in its text (Figure 4.1). Surely it can't be meant to go at a sober four-count with all those repeated notes. How fast can it go? Let's find out. How quickly can you enunciate the text? (Don't forget a thoroughly backwoods pronunciation with modified vowels and elided syllables.) How many accents are there in a measure? For a rousing square dance, we need a firm beat, and there's only time for one in each measure. So the time signature should honestly be 1/1 rather than 2/2 or 4/4.

FIGURE 4.1. "Weevily Wheat"

Oh, Char-ley he's a fine young man, Char-ley, he's a

dan-dy; Char-ley likes to kiss the girls, and he can do it

Refrain

han-dy.—— I don't want none of your wee-vi-ly wheat. I

don't want none of your bar-ley. I want fine flour in

half an hour, to bake a cake for Char-ley.——

Text and tune: American traditional

At this speed, and with this unyielding series of accents, there's not much chance for subtlety of movement. But the singer has words and a face. The combination of teasing exaggeration and mock indignation lends varied tones of voice. Ideally, the verse should be sung in one breath, and the only spot for rhythmic play is in the extension of the final note, which might be different for each verse and refrain.

Can you hear a quick banjo pickin' the tune? Or a drone accompaniment? Or a lone fiddle, weaving arabesques around the phrases? When we find the right tempo, sonority, mood, and function, other ideas come crowding in. It's like unlocking Pandora's box, only this time it's full of good things, creative ideas that sustain and build momentum for the song.

I spoke above of meter and the number of accents in one bar. Here is another instance of the inadequacy of our notation. If we always read 4/4 to mean a strong accent on one and a lesser one on three, we're stuck with 4/4 = march. But if we realize that the music can be immensely varied within 4/4, we can play with accents, one each bar or every other bar. Or we can change accents to go with word stresses. Or combine both of these techniques to give the suggestion of "march" under "love song."

Let us think about time and its relationship to one song. There is no way the song can be separated from time. It occupies a swatch of time as a painting occupies space. The real question is how this particular song fills that space. The choices are basic. Is the time metered or free (e.g., speech rhythms)? If the latter, how free? Is it different each time? Is there no hint of regularity? If metered, is it duple or triple? The difference between these is important.

> *Exercise*: Imagine you are holding a tennis ball in your hand. Now drop it on a count of one and catch it on two, several times. Change the pattern to drop it on one and catch it on three. You'll feel the emphasis in your wrist much more on this because it takes more energy to propel the ball far enough to cover the extra count. Triple patterns need stronger first-beat accents than duple.

"Soldier, Soldier" (Figure 4.2) is an atypical march. It begins with a nice jaunty duple rhythm and all of a sudden there comes a triple; those two alternate for a bit. I like to hear the steady march under the shifting accents as the voice moves from the woman's question to the refrain ("for O the fife and drum") and to the man's reply.

FIGURE 4.2. "Soldier, Soldier"

Text and tune: British and American traditional

FIGURE 4.3. "Herr Jesu Christ"

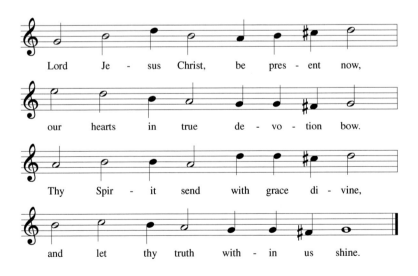

Text: Wilhelm II, 1598–1662, tr. Catherine Winkwork, 1829–1878, alt.
The Chorale Book for England, 1863
Tune: *Cantionale Germanicum Dresden*, 1628

Here is a different way to play with twos and threes. Although the words of "Herr Jesu Christ" (Figure 4.3) are cheerfully sacred, the rhythms are those of a very popular Renaissance dance, alternating 6/4 and 3/2 measures. Sing the rhythms, making each syllable the same length:

3 and ‖: 1 and a 2 and a   1 and 2 and 3 and :‖ (4x)

Feel in your body the alternation of twos and threes until it becomes easy and natural. Then start moving across the floor, feeling strong accents on each first beat.

This is known as a complex meter because of the double motion: 6/4 has two beats of three pulses, and 3/2 has three beats of two pulses. Others are 5/8 (2 + 3 or 3 + 2) and 7/8 (3 + 2 + 2 or 2 + 3 + 2 or 2 + 2+ 3) Try dancing them! Figure 4.4 is a lively African hymn in 7/8:

FIGURE 4.4. "Kinga Tune"

Text: Tanzanian traditional, Swahili, tr. Howard S. Olson copyright © 1977
Tune: Copyright © 1977 Howard Olson

Of course, there are as many variations of twos and threes as there are motions of the human body to illustrate them—each song inhabits its own universe of pulse, accent, and tempo. Sensing the variables within the song, rather than adhering to what is predictable, leads to idiomatic and expressive performance. For example, we generally think of tempo as rigidly unbending, as in a strongly accented dance. In actual practice, however, there is flexibility, not only where a slowing or speeding up is indicated, but even where a strong accent is needed, which is accomplished by the slight delay of the pulse. My visual image is of a dancer swirling around the stage coming to a leap—which needs more time. In fact, if the pulse is metronomically steady at moments like this, all the kinetic dramatic sense is lost. Another kind of flexibility is that freedom accorded to singers who must fit many kinds of consonants into the given pattern. Most of the time these variations are so subtle that they are not indicated on the page—and those who accompany the dancer or singer usually put some mark on the page as a reminder: a comma, fermata, or a more individual sign.

Ponder the variations possible within a plain duple meter with no change of tempo. FOUNDATION is an early American hymn tune usually notated in a straightforward 4/4 and sung rather like a march (Figure 4.5).

Imagine singing at about half note = 60, first to an accompaniment of sixteenth notes, then eighths, then quarters, then half notes, then wholes, then double-wholes. We move from notes that must be dropped with great precision into their sixteenth-note slots to notes that stretch with broad *legato* into widely separated accents. It's as though we were looking a few inches ahead, then a few feet, then some yards, and, finally, as far as we can see. The specific note values get less and less important, and the breadth of the phrase—the sense of eternity—takes over. I call this kind of beat a pendulum beat; a heavy weight is held aloft until it accumulates a huge amount of energy and then falls with enormous power into an arc, which results in another momentary pause before the next inevitable downswing.

FIGURE 4.5. FOUNDATION

Text: J. Rippon's *A Selection of Hymns*, 1787
Tune: Joseph Funk's *Compilation of Genuine Church Music*, 1832

Another possibility for variation is found in the rhythmic modes that developed in the medieval period. They suggest that in a melody that moves in equal pulses, it is possible to lengthen some notes to change the meter. Thus "Twinkle, Twinkle" is usually sung in a regular 2/4.

"Twin-kle, twin-kle lit-tle star."
 1 2 1 2 1 2 1 2

But it could be 3/4:

"Twin-kle, twin-kle lit- tle star." (long/short)
 12 3 12 3 12 3 1 2 3

Or another 3/4:

"Twin-kle, twin- kle lit- tle   star." (short/long)
  1   23   1   23 1   23   1 2 3

And we could even put it in a very modern 5/4, three beats on "Twin" and two on "kle":

"Twin-kle, Twin-kle   lit- tle   star."____
1 2 3 4 5 1 2 3 4 5   123 4 5   1 2 3 4 5

In Chapter 1, I covered music in which the basic pulse is free. Such music is not difficult to sing in the same manner as we speak it and is readily learned by ear. (It is impossible to notate.) When well performed, it creates music of incredible serenity and mystery, as exemplified in the ancient Gregorian chants. Somehow the addition of pitches to beautifully spoken free speech rhythms seems to release us into empyrean realms of pure spirit. There are soaring examples from all around the world, melodies that explore moods impossible to arrive at through metric schemes. These, too, are a form of dance; look at the lovely gestures that invoke it.

FIGURE 4.6. Chant text from *Liber Usualis*—spoken stresses

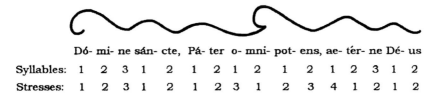

Dó- mi- ne sán- cte, Pá- ter o- mni- pot- ens, ae- tér- ne Dé- us
Syllables: 1 2 3 1 2 1 2 1 2 1 2 1 2 3 1 2
Stresses: 1 2 3 1 2 1 2 3 1 2 3 4 1 2 1 2

So the dance of rhythm, of music, continues unbroken. It will never die as long as there is one human body to respond to it, and it is born again with each new child. It is the relationship of our bodies to the stream of time. The more that we are aware of our participation in the cosmic dance, the more we are transported by its energy.

— REFLECTIONS —

Finding the dance—"Weevily Wheat" (Figure 4.1):

- Sing the song as if you were accompanying a square dance.
- Now think the song, and become a dancer. Allow your body to move in response to the song.
- Try it slow, medium, fast, faster.
- Move arms, legs, shoulders, hips, everything.

  Are you gliding along the floor or bouncing off of it?

  Are you covering lots of space, a little, or none?

  Are you moving in curves, straight lines, or circles?

- Analyze how your body expresses rhythms, the words, the tune.

  Have you ever participated in a square dance?

  Can you imagine how this one would look?

- How important are the words in this song to the dance? What happens to the dance when you run out of words?
- Sing it as:

  A courting song

  A children's game song

  A girl exasperated with Charley

  A girl who will put up with almost anything from Charley

  Total nonsense

  Which do you like best? Why?

More verses for "Weevily Wheat" (Figure 4.1—p. 33):

Coffee grows on white oak trees,
River flows with brandy;
Choose you one to roam with you
Sweet as 'lasses candy.

Charley's here and Charley's there,
Charley's over the ocean.
Charley, he'll come back some day,
Unless he takes a notion!

More verses for "Herr Jesu Christ" (Figure 4.3):

Unseal our lips to sing thy praise,
Our souls to thee in worship raise,
Make strong our faith, increase our light
That we may know thy name aright.

Till we with saints in glad accord
Sing "Holy, holy, is the Lord!"
And in the light of heav'n above
Shall see thy face and know thy love.

CHAPTER 5:
THE USES OF SILENCE

RESTS IN MUSIC denote silence—but this is far from empty space. Silence is the necessary partner of sound; the two together create one whole. Where rests are not written, they are implied at the beginnings and endings of sound. One of the worst transgressions of our electronic media is the turning of silence into a negative value. (*It's not working.*) In our media, speaking overlaps into music into more music often overlaid with noise. But for true music-making, silence itself is the frame.

In a wonderful book called *The Silence of God*, James P. Carse posits two kinds of silence: empty and fulfilled. Applied biblically, this can refer to whatever existed before the creation of the universe and what will be after the last judgment. Musically, is the space empty before the piece begins? Not in a concert hall, in the expectant hush before the sounds. This rest is full of anticipation. Is it empty when the sound ceases? No, here is true fulfilled silence, echoing with preceding strains, full as our bodies are after a meal.

Take the beginning silence one step further. At the start of Beethoven's Fifth Symphony, there is the famous motif: three short notes and one long note. But look and listen closely (Figure 5.1). The first indication in the score is an eighth rest. What is the difference between the expectant silence and that charged millisecond at the conductor's downbeat?

FIGURE 5.1. Ludwig van Beethoven's Fifth Symphony—initial theme

Bach's *Well-Tempered Klavier* provides other examples. He was a master of fitting the phrase into the larger implied metric pattern. Look at Book II, Fugue No. 14 in F-sharp minor, where the theme enters on the second half of beat two in common time. Not until the fourth measure do we get a note sounded on the downbeat. The measured silence at the start is absolutely necessary for the performer to create the flow that can carry the listening ear over to that downbeat.

FIGURE 5.2. J. S. Bach's *Well-Tempered Klavier II*—Fugue No. 14

Recording engineers know the importance of getting enough "room sound" at the beginning and end of each take. This is far from empty space. One cannot substitute the silence of one room for another or for the deadness of blank tape.

Rests in vocal music often convey the breath that separates one phrase from another, as well as listening time between one phrase and its answer. Composers use rests in many different, often characteristic, ways. In the arrangements I completed with Robert Shaw, rests often denote the exact placement of a final consonant, as well as the intake of breath for the beginning of a new phrase. (I remember the argument with a copy editor over a rest with an accent on it, which I thought was perfectly logical—then and now.) And in an extreme instance, I have notated two full measures of rest in a slow tempo before the final resolution of a long work (Figure 5.3). How do I come to that decision? I am conducting all the time I compose, and this helps me to solve many duration problems. I try to listen to where the music wants to go at the same time as I gently guide it toward my plan.

FIGURE 5.3. *Songs for Eve*—ending of the last movement

Tune: Copyright © 1976 Alice Parker

And then there's CALVARY (Figure 5.4). This spiritual also begins with an eighth rest, but what a difference from Beethoven! It is one of the most haunting melodies I know, wedding an incantatory repetition of the word to the musical phrase.

FIGURE 5.4. CALVARY

Text and tune: African American spiritual

The accented rest launches the melody as the down-step of the diver launches the body into the air. Three steps up and then a long way down, essentially repeated three times with a fourth phrase that is only the downward movement extended into a low cadence on the final syllable. These pitch curves generate an enormous amount of energy, which is heightened by the continual third-beat rests.

Another lesson about these initial rests came years later, as I used the melody in a group improvisation. My downbeat became stronger and stronger until it turned into a whip, the lash that prompts an anguished reply. This time an entire roomful of people felt that spell. We were reduced to singing only the word "Calvary" over and over till the song finally ended. Years later that memory is still vivid.

One more word about the use and non-use of rests: our hymnals generally use no rests. Someone told me once that was a decision made in the nineteenth century by editors who thought the page looked too busy or confusing. This policy leads to the absurdity of a whole note tied over to a quarter note with the next phrase beginning on beat two. A rest on that first beat would not only look neater; it is also a signal to the singer that a breath has to be taken on that beat. Perhaps if we rethought this policy, the rhythmic integrity of our congregational singing might improve.

But I believe we should use rests in this way only in music that is metered. They really don't belong in chant. There is no symbol in Gregorian notation for silence, only the slight verticals used to denote different kinds of phrase endings. Here I much prefer the use of a comma, which does not impose an implied length on the breath-time. But even this gentle rule is impossible for me to use consistently. It's another indication of the difficulty of notating the language we use every day, not only its sounds, but also its silences.

— REFLECTIONS —

Silence:

- A rest in music never indicates emptiness. There is always something going on: energy gathering or dispersing, a breath being taken, a dance pausing or continuing through the momentary absence of sound. Listen for the quality of the silence.
- In CALVARY (Figure 5.4) the refrain is simply the repetition of the word twice on each phrase until the last line: "Surely he died on Calvary." Think the image of the whip: the gathering of energy as the body prepares for the "snap!" (rather like lightning), then the recovery, so the rhythmic cycle can begin again. Compare this with the energy of the sung phrase.

Beat:	3	4	1	2	3	4	1	2	3	4
Whip:	>				>				>	
			>				>			
Voice:		Cal - va - ry_____			Cal - va - ry_____				etc.	

- Be aware of the reciprocal action going on between the whip and the song, each complementing the other and spurring each other on.
- Now try the image of a chain gang, men working with heavy hammers, breaking rock. What is the difference in the quality of the accent? Can you think of another image?
- Here is another kind of silence to ponder. As we sing, we sustain principally the vowel sounds. Some consonants are pitched (e.g., "m" and "n" can be sustained; "b," "d," and "g" are voiced but cannot be sustained). But some have no pitch quality at all: in essence, they create a kind of silence. Listen for the interruptions at "s," "h," and "c" as you speak or sing: **S**urely **h**e died on **C**alvary.

Sometimes I think these are the most expressive of all consonants. Are their silences individually different? What are other unvoiced consonants?

Here is a different example:

FIGURE 5.5. "I Got Rhythm"

Music and Lyrics by George Gershwin and Ira Gershwin copyright ©1930 WB Music Corp. (Renewed) Gershwin® and George Gershwin® are registered trademarks of Gershwin Enterprises. All Rights Reserved.

- What is the difference between songs that begin on the beat and off the beat?
- Look at other examples in this book. All the reflections at the end of each chapter can be applied to any song you sing.

—THE POOL OF SILENCE—

Deep in the shadowed woods lies a small pool, perhaps eight feet across. It is almost a perfect circle, silent, surrounded by pebbled, mossy banks. One leaf falls, and ripples radiate out, beginning in a burst of energy, then slowly dissipating as they touch the shore. More leaves fall, creating an elaborate pattern of tiny waves on the surface, each with a source, following its own energies in a complex dance. They create a miniature storm of intersecting energies, then ebb as gently as they began. The pool is quiet again: timeless, motionless, waiting.

Silence is the frame for music.

CHAPTER 6:
MOUNTAIN RANGES

WHEN WE LISTEN to a melody, we are not usually conscious of individual pitches or the specific intervals making up the line. I, at least, hear a succession of curves, or arcs rising and falling, usually reaching a climax at some point and most often falling down to a close. In other words, pitches heard are relative to each other, to the home note, to the range of the performer's voice. There is nothing fixed about them until we try to write them down or play them on a keyed instrument.

As we discuss pitch, let us keep hearing living music—a human voice, say—rather than visualizing a page or a keyboard or an electronic beep. These have little if any emotional affect, and I want to consider pitch in its most human context.

Each culture has its own way of using pitches. The physical fact that the first overtone is half the number of vibrations of the foundation tone is true everywhere. In Western music we call this an octave, but only because somehow we divided the space into seven notes, or eight steps. But there are many other ways of subdividing the octave; a worldwide favorite seems to be the pentatonic, or five-note, scale exemplified by the black notes on the piano. This gapped scale is found in Asian, African, and Eastern European music as well as music of many other cultures. Think of it as a scale constructed of five rising consecutive fifths. Or think of it as deriving from the universal childhood chant based on three of the five notes (Figure 6.1).

FIGURE 6.1. "Olly, Olly In-free"

Ol - ly Ol - ly   in - free.

The seven-note major and minor scales took over in seventeenth-century European music, and we are taught that these are the norm. I'd rather consider them an offshoot of the norm, a sophisticated kind of writing that developed with the onset of notation and printing. Tonality (a home note including a major scale and its triads) is differentiated from modality (still a seven-note scale, but without chordal implications). These two systems are branches of the tree of world music, but not necessarily the most important ones.

Scales are theoretical constructs. Songs are not. Songs use exactly as much of any scale as they need and no more. They go as high or low as they need, in as many phrases as they need. One of the first things to notice about a song is exactly which pitches it uses, not assuming that because it sounds major it uses all the notes of a major scale. Each song is complete unto itself; resist the urge to standardize.

An interval is the distance between two pitches, either consecutive or simultaneous. Our system of defining them by half steps (from each note on the piano to its closest neighbor) is sadly limiting. This adds up to what we call a chromatic scale of twelve half steps. This can't account for blue notes, for the raised leading tone, or the expressive, flat descending whole tone. An electronic tuning device has 100 cents between C and D, 100 possible gradations of pitch. How many do we use? Other cultures? A violinist as opposed to a harpist? A blues singer as opposed to a classical soprano?

Bach is a pertinent name here, for he carried to completion in living sound the idea of equal semitones between the whole steps of the scale. This allows F-sharp to equal G-flat and the whole world of modulation to open up—the world of specifically harmonic language as opposed to merely melodic or rhythmic. But we are examining mere melody in this book, and the tunes far antedate the theories. Look at the following examples.

"Poor Wayfaring Stranger" (Figure 6.2) is a traditional melody using only five pitches, but there is no feeling of deprivation—just the rise and fall of a beautifully crafted song. It is all within the compass of a fifth until the second half. Then it moves up from its previous high to the upper octave three phrases in a row before repeating the first-half cadence. What a lovely song for the voice to sing with its repeated initial notes and its melancholy wanderings.

FIGURE 6.2. "Poor Wayfaring Stranger"—pentatonic version

Text and tune: American traditional

This first example is what I call a minor pentatonic; its home is definitely on *la* rather than *do*. (By constructing scales on five different home tones we get five different pentatonics, so even within this restricted scale we find amazing variety.) I happen to prefer another version of the same song, this time in a modal aeolian hexatonic (six-note) scale (Figure 6.3).

FIGURE 6.3. "Poor Wayfaring Stranger"—modal version

Text and tune: American traditional

Next is a far more complex example from the Appalachian Mountains with deep roots in the folklore of the British Isles. "He's Gone Away" begins with an abrupt rise, almost an arm waving goodbye, and then goes up once more before subsiding reluctantly home. Its answering curve is gentler, returning us to the modal home note on a subtly altered pentatonic scale (Figure 6.4).

FIGURE 6.4. "He's Gone Away"—refrain

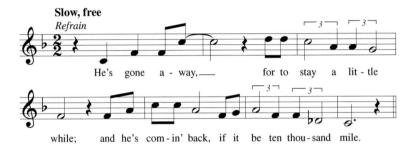

He's gone a-way, for to stay a lit-tle while; and he's com-in' back, if it be ten thou-sand mile.

Text and tune: American traditional

I hear this refrain almost as a chant. It moves ahead and then holds back; the long notes can be held still longer, and there's no hurry from phrase to phrase.

The verses are different (Figure 6.5). They move much more purposefully and rhythmically with a sequence of questions, until arriving at the climactic "kiss" (which should surely be held) before slipping back into the free rhythms of the refrain.

The full song, as notated by Carl Sandburg in *The American Songbag*, is distinguished by still another set of verses that must be true free recitative (Figure 6.6). They center on that age-old children's cry noted in Figure 6.1 and should come from the heart. (Is it possible that each measure should be about the same length? Tap a slow, unchanging one and stretch or squeeze the words to fit.)

FIGURE 6.5. "He's Gone Away"—verses

Text and tune: American traditional

The whole adds up to a veritable aria of love, courtship, separation, and longing with a very contemporary freedom of musical form and content, including the enigmatic brief coda. The song gives an initial impression of being pentatonic, which is first contradicted by the flatted penultimate note, sounding almost like blues. The next stretch is at the word "glove," which is then topped by the raised tone on "kiss"—balanced by the flatted tone on "is"—which becomes almost chromatic. Except that the tune is anything but chromatic! It is its own individual blend of different scales, rhythms, thoughts, and forms, which add up to an unforgettable experience. Sandburg places it first in his collection.

What is the home note of the song? Our tonal ears insist on *do*, wanting to end the song on "over Yandro." But Sandburg ends it the modal way, on "miles." That may sound unfinished to ears with tonal expectations—but that is characteristic of many modal melodies. Another way of naming those pentatonic scales above would be the modal way (e.g., dorian, phrygian, etc.)—the pretonal way.

FIGURE 6.6. "He's Gone Away"—"On Yandro's high hill..."

Text and tune: American traditional

So the major scale, in which most music has been sung since the Baroque period, just happens to be the one mode that took over, crowding out all the others except the aeolian, or minor, and even influencing that to veer closer and closer to major. When I find songs with these altered minor notes, I often try singing in the natural minor. Sometimes it works wonderfully well at giving the impression that this is the way the song is most at home.

In my book *Creative Hymn Singing*, there's an example of a beautiful, old-as-the-hills sounding dorian tune that leans on and repeats the tritone (F to B) that can characterize this scale (Figure 6.7). Notice that this tune is hexatonic, six notes only.

FIGURE 6.7. "O Thou in Whose Presence"–modal

Oh, thou, in whose pre - sence my soul takes de - light, on whom in af-

flic - tion I call,——— my com - fort by day,— and my

song in the night, my hope, my sal - va - tion, my all.———

Text: Joseph Swain, 1791
Tune: A. M. Buchanan, *Folk Hymns of America*, 1938

Now sing it again, changing all the F-naturals to F-sharps (Figure 6.8). With the change of only five notes, the whole mood of the song has been altered from wistful longing to confident statement, from modal scale to major.

FIGURE 6.8. "O Thou in Whose Presence"—F-sharp added

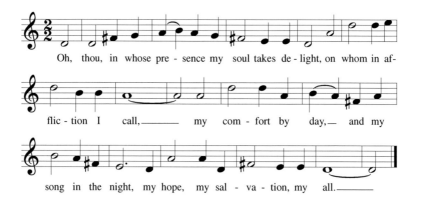

Oh, thou, in whose pre - sence my soul takes de - light, on whom in af-

flic - tion I call,——— my com - fort by day,— and my

song in the night, my hope, my sal - va - tion, my all.———

Tune: attr. Freeman Lewis, 1813

In the following variant the missing seventh step is restored, triumphantly making the half step leading tone demanded by complete major scales (Figure 6.9). We've moved from perhaps the fifteenth century to a sturdy late nineteenth-century rural hymn tune.

FIGURE 6.9. "O Thou in Whose Presence"—leading tone added

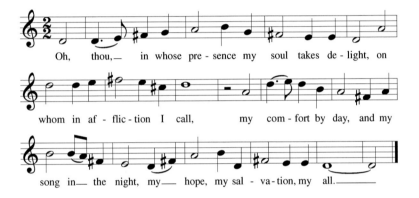

Tune: J. Funk, *A Compilation of Genuine Church Music*, 1835

When we truly listen, pitches are as hard to quantify as the whole field of rhythm. One singer may use different tunings in different songs or sing with bent pitches in blues or Eastern melodies. This sensitivity can lead to the wonderful, mysterious, unmeasurable occurrences characteristic of great performances. If our ears are open, we cannot only hear them, but echo them in our own minds and voices. These are the minute details that distinguish one singer from another, as well as the possibilities that exist within the seed of each song. Not only is song "that-which-cannot-be-notated," but each melody is as triumphantly individual as a single oak tree or daisy.

— REFLECTIONS —

Mountain Ranges—"Poor Wayfaring Stranger" (Figures 6.2–6.3) "He's Gone Away" (Figures 6.4–6.6), "O Thou, in Whose Presence" (Figures 6.7–6.9):

- Begin by identifying the home note and the scale. Then draw in the air the curve of each phrase. Notice the relationship of one phrase to another, the high point and the low point and how they relate to the home note. Is most of the melody above it? Below it? Circling around it?

- The most vocal part of the song is the way it feels in the throat of the singer. It takes more energy to rise than to fall. Feel that energy lifting the phrase and gently dissipating as it comes down.

- What kind of sound is right for the top note? The lowest note?

- What is the dynamic scale you are working in? Wide? Narrow?

- How does your voice relate to the style of the piece?
    Is your voice Classical? Folk? Popular? Other? (Can you name it?)
    Is the song Classical? Folk? Popular? Other?

- How do you bridge the gap?

- To whom are you singing? A child? A parent? A friend? A stranger? A group? Are they next to you? Far away? How far?

- Where are you singing? In a concert hall? A living room? Outdoors?

- Is the space resonant? Dead? In between?

- How do you adjust to the space? Do you sing the same way no matter what or where you are singing?

- Look back at all the songs we've studied so far. How do you change your voice from "He's Gone Away" to "Weevily Wheat"?

- Is there a real difference between metric pieces and free pieces? A free rhythm allows lots of time for vowels, for breathing, and for vocalizing the phrase. A steady meter usually cuts short the vowel, emphasizing the consonants. The beat is more important than the word rhythms, and the result is more instrumental, more concerned with attacks than with sustainings. The consonants provide rhythmic articulation. See the difference in the melodic curves between a metered and a free version of "He's Gone Away":

FIGURE 6.10. "He's Gone Away"—melodic curves

Metric curves

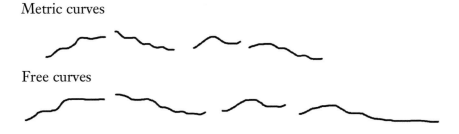

Free curves

—PATTERNS IN SONG MATERIALS—

Texts:

> syllable or accent count
>
> poetic schemes
>
> rhyme schemes
>
> figures of speech

Rhythms:

> tempo
>
> meters: duple, triple, mixed, beginning on the beat, beginning with an upbeat
>
> quality of beat (what kind of motion)

Pitches:

> home note (usually final *do* in major)
>
> scale (organization within an octave)
>
>> notes actually used in a song
>>
>> pentatonic (five-note gapped scale)
>>
>>> home on *do* or *re* or *mi* or *sol* or *la*
>>
>> modal (seven-note whole and half steps)
>>
>>> home on *re* or *mi* or *fa* or *sol* or *la* or *do*
>>
>> tonal (seven-note whole and half steps)
>>
>>> major = 1 1 ½ 1 1 1 ½ (home on *do*)
>>>
>>>> minor = 1 ½ 1 1 ½ 1 1 (home on *la*)
>>>
>>>> with *fa*, or *fa* and *sol*, pulling toward major
>>
>> ethnic (non-Western)
>>
>> motion up, down, or static; step or skip
>>
>>> away from and returning to home

Forms:

    phrase

        length, range, motion, tension,

        balance, question and answer

    cadence

        home, away (how far away?)

    repetition and contrast (ABA)

    tension, climax, release

Articulation:

    notes connected or separated (*staccato-legato*)

Dynamics:

    soft to loud (***pp–ff***)

Mood:

    rage/sorrow to elation/joy

THE EXPLOSIVE COMBINATION:

MELODY

Chapter 7:
Breath and Phrase

THE BUILDING BLOCKS of text, rhythm, and pitch we have been discussing are here woven into one whole: the song itself. The basic unit of the combination is the phrase, the smallest element of musical thought. Just as in the English language, the phrase expresses an idea, and several phrases can make up the equivalent of a sentence or a paragraph.

Phrases begin and end with an intake of breath, and their length is often determined by this physical limitation. Breath is to the singer as the floor is to the dancer. There is no way to escape this human necessity. It is woven into the fabric of all song.

Have you ever tried to define a phrase? Here are some of my attempts. A phrase is a memorable unit (one can remember it because it fits together). Phrases are what you breathe at the end of. Phrases are the smallest units that, added together, make a melody.

One phrase may be compared to another in regard to length, range, motion, tension, and balance. Phrases may also be compared in terms of repetition and contrast.

A phrase has three parts: beginning, middle, and end. (It's astonishing how many students forget this elementary wisdom when beginning to read and write.) The end is easiest to recognize: it's where you breathe. Then comes a beginning, and the middle progresses in a satisfying way to the next cadence or ending.

There are as many varieties of endings in music as there are there are in language. While written English has commas and periods, colons and semicolons, question marks and exclamation points, the spoken language has an infinite number of very subtle pauses. And music shares that possibility. Compare the phrase endings in the next song: Which are really final? Are there some that are almost final (that is, the song must continue)? Are some equivalent to commas? Are any two exactly equal in weight? And think how different this tune sounds when different people sing it. There are almost infinitely variable combinations of pitches and rhythms, beginnings and endings, pauses and completions.

The structure of a song is revealed in its phrases. Look at the words of this familiar hymn. Note that there are only three lines in the text of the poem, wonderfully extended with interjections ("O my soul") and repetitions. Here is the verbal text without repetitions:

What wondrous love is this,
O my soul,
That caused the Lord of bliss
To bear the dreadful curse
For my soul.

Listen for the way that the music weaves the repetitions into a seamless whole.

FIGURE 7.1. WONDROUS LOVE

What won-drous love is this, O my soul, O my soul! What

won-drous love is this, O my soul! What won-drous love is

this that caused the Lord of bliss to bear the dread-ful curse for my

soul, for my soul, to bear the dread-ful curse for my soul.

Text: American folk hymn, ca. 1835
Tune: *The Southern Harmony*, 1835

Another way of expressing the musical form would be in terms of the number of syllables in each phrase:

music phrase:	1	2	3	4	5	6
text line:	1	1	1	2	3	3
music repetition:	A	B	C	D	A	B
syllable count:	6 3 3	6 3	6	6	6 3 3	6 3
or:	12	9	6	6	12	9

The complexity of the structure is revealed even more through the realization that the first two lines are echoed in the last two, but the third line of the poem is sung to the same melody as the first line of the song. There are overlappings upon overlappings. Interwoven with the text repetition is the pitch structure. The first big curve takes us from home to the step above. The second rises higher and falls back to home. The third rises highest of all and ends there. The fourth falls all the way home. The fifth and sixth repeat the first and second.

FIGURE 7.2. WONDROUS LOVE—melodic curves

All this sounds very technical. And one need not know any of it to sing the song or to enjoy the hearing of it. But it's fascinating to discover that there is a multiplicity of subtle interweavings here that create a structure of incredible tensile strength. One can trust this song implicitly. It will not fail you. And I've not mentioned the central mystery of the text, or the modal scale that sounds old as the hills, or the inward questioning of the text reinforced by its "lonesome tune" quality, or the transformation into affirmation at the end. It's no wonder we don't know who wrote it! It sounds as if it had been created on Day One.

Knowing the structure of the song, analyzing and diagramming it, helps us to see how it works. All this is an aid to memory, to expressivity, to knowing where you are in the song as you perform it. It's exactly analogous to a road map. We may have driven many times to a nearby town, but there's a shock of altered perception when we find it on a map or see it in an aerial photograph. The road doesn't change, but our perception of it does.

And just as repeated travels on a difficult road make it familiar, so it is with music. As composers and performers, it behooves us to know where we are in the piece as we bring it to life so we can balance all these complex interweavings into one whole.

— REFLECTIONS —

Breath and phrase:

- We find examples of phrase lengths, patterns, and cadences in every song we sing. Breath is inextricably woven into song, and deciding where and where not to breathe is part of the singer's art. If we try to erect a framework for comparing songs, it might look like this:

    1) Key, meter, tempo, motion, mood, function
    2) Text: the number of syllables per line of poetry; rhyme scheme, number of verses, speakers; musical structure scheme (repetitions)
    3) Pitch: home note, scale, curves, cadences (how much finality?)

Example:

"Oh, Shenandoah" (Figure 1.1):

1) **key:** E-flat, **meter:** 4/4, **tempo:** slow, **motion:** free, **mood:** remembered love, **function:** fo'castle shanty

2) **number of syllables per line of poetry:**
   4 + 5 solo, 7 ref. *a*, 4 + 5 solo, 6 ref. *b*, 6 ref. *c*
   rhyme scheme, number of verses, speakers:
   abacd, 3 verses, solo/group
   music structural scheme (repetitions):
   ABCDE (no repetitions)

3) **home note:** E-flat, **scale:** E-flat major
   curves and cadences (how much finality?):

ascend up an octave, query, to 5; bold curves	away
response, descend from high E-flat to 5	away
query, descend from C to 1	close, but not home
response, ascend up to 5	away
final response, rise and fall to 1	home

"In Balinderry" (Figure 3.1):

1) **key:** D, **meter:** 6/8, **tempo:** medium, **motion:** metric,
   mood: remembered love, **function:** spinning song
2) **number of syllables per line of poetry:**
   10 9 11 8 // 10 10 8 9
   rhyme scheme, number of verses, speakers:
   abcb ccdd, 2 verses (here), woman (narrator)
   music structural scheme (repetitions):
   AABC AABC
3) **home note:** D, **scale:** D major (no seventh)
   curves and cadences (how much finality?):

3 up to 5 down to 1'; gentle curves	not full stop
repeat but end on 3	almost full stop
5 down to 1 and up to 6'	really away
5 down to 1 up to 3 down to 1	really home

More verses for WONDROUS LOVE
(Figure 7.1—p. 69):

> When I was sinking down, sinking down',
> When I was sinking down,
> Beneath God's righteous frown,
> Christ laid aside his crown for my soul.

> To God and to the Lamb I will sing,
> To God and to the Lamb,
> Who is the great I AM,
> While millions join the theme, I will sing.

> And when from death I'm free, I'll sing on;
> And when from death I am free
> I'll sing and joyful be,
> And through eternity I'll sing on.

Chapter 8:
Text and Tune—Marital Alliances

SOME SONGS SPRING whole from the same source. Music and words are born together and destined never to part. The old black spirituals are excellent examples. Who can imagine singing a different text to the tune of "Swing Low, Sweet Chariot"? Others form incredibly sensitive unions though divided by place and time. The example below (Figure 8.1) unites a brief eighteenth-century poem by Alexander Pope with a tune named WALLINGFORD in a nineteenth-century Connecticut oblong hymnal.

Figure 8.1. WALLINGFORD

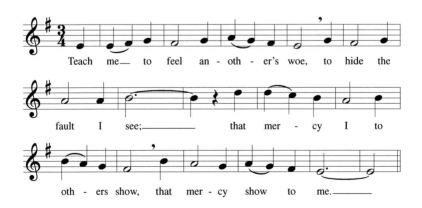

Text: Alexander Pope
Tune: WALLINGFORD, Connecticut, 19th c.

And still other pairings are arranged marriages: the tune is written for a preexisting text, or vice versa. Think of the incredible artistry of George and Ira Gershwin, which allowed either one to supply one element for the other to complete, in either order.

Most fickle of all are hymn tunes. They are often engaged in a whole series of alliances. Some are remarkably good. I think of the sturdy Scottish Psalter tunes and the Welsh HYFRYDOL, which seems to ennoble each text with which it is sung (Figure 8.2).

FIGURE 8.2. HYFRYDOL

Tune: Rowland Hugh Prichard, 1811–1887

But I can't think of a text that might ennoble any tune. This brings us to the question: What is the nature of this alliance? Who dominates? Why are some better than others? How does one judge?

Let's look at an old example (Figure 8.3). The tune O WALY, WALY comes from the British Isles and is found in this form in the Southern Appalachians.

FIGURE 8.3. "The Water Is Wide"

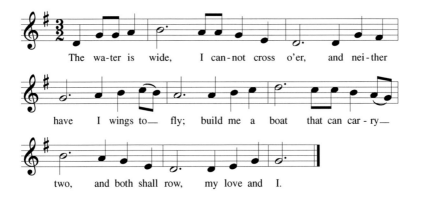

The wa-ter is wide, I can-not cross o'er, and nei-ther have I wings to— fly; build me a boat that can car-ry— two, and both shall row, my love and I.

Text and tune: O WALY, WALY, British Isles

O love is handsome and love is kind
Gay as a jewel when first it's new,
But love grows old and waxes cold
And fades away like the morning dew.

O waly, waly up the bank
And waly, waly down the brae,
And waly, waly by yon burn side
Where me and my love were wont to gae.

These are only a few of the many verses of this ballad. Both words and tune have been altered over the centuries, planed down to fit the local language and voice. But the timeless story of true love turned false has endeared it to generations of folksingers, and for good reason. This is a seamless match of text and tune, its melody rising and falling in sensuous curves. Odd syllables in the text need to be fitted into the lines: true folksingers have no difficulty with this, even adding beats or notes to accommodate the text. Both elements continually support each other, the abiding tune and the changing words constantly enriching each other and the whole.

Placing such a widely known tune into a hymnal is a dangerous undertaking. If the theme of the poem is radically changed, there is a tension between the remembered focus and the new. One hymnal supplement supplies a text that begins "An upper room did my Lord prepare." The jump from spurned love to Passion Week is too much for me to compass. Another attempt, which works more easily, places the song at a wedding with references both to young love and to the trials it may be facing: "When love is found and hope comes home." But even this feels slightly uncomfortable; the emotion, qualified by religious undertones, is not so elemental as in the original.

Fun songs like "My Bonnie" (Figure 8.4) invite endless improvisation in both text and tune. The basic materials are light

FIGURE 8.4. "My Bonnie"

Text and tune: Scottish traditional

stuff—"marshmallows" is the technical term—and give way with good humor to verbal and musical maulings that would be unthinkable with more serious models. We must remember, however, that this song has persisted for at least a century. What is there about its inner relationships that give it such longevity?

Translations pose their own hazards. If they follow the sense of the original closely, it's almost certain that the English will be in a peculiar order, or not flowing along with the tune. Here is a brief example: three texts to one phrase from the first chorus in Felix Mendelssohn's *Elijah* (Figure 8.5). The first is the original German, the second is the traditional English translation, and the third is my own attempt to put "help" in the right place.

FIGURE 8.5. Felix Mendelssohn's *Elijah*—translations

und uns ist kei - ne Hül - fe ge - kom - men (original German)
and yet no po - wer com - eth to help us (published translation)
and yet our cries for help go un - an - swered (Alice Parker translation)

(Note the "k" and "h" sounds in "keine Hülfe" and "cries for help.")

Hymns suffer particularly from this failure to pair effectively. There seems to be a feeling that if the words are talking about something holy, that is enough. For the discriminating singer, that is certainly not true: a careless text can reduce even a wonderful melody to ruins. Choosing by syllable count (the meter of hymns) is basic but much more important is the nature of the tune (its mood, function, voice, tone) and the comfort level of the combination. (I ask the tune questions: Is that all right? Does this text really belong to you?)

Hymnals are full of bad marriages, and our sensitivities get dulled by constant exposure to bad models. (Think of the tune of "A Mighty

Fortress Is Our God" sung to "In Unity We Lift Our Song." The idea is fine; the strong accent on the last syllable of "unity" is not.) Try consulting the metrical index in the back of any hymnal and look up the text for the first example in any meter. Then try that text with each of the succeeding metrically matched melodies in turn. They should all fit, but you'll find that few of them do. The big difference is, of course, whether the song or poem begins on a strong beat or an upbeat. But after that there's a very real sense of belonging or not belonging. It's amazing how few are really good combinations.

When hymns are selected by text, the suitability of the tune is usually ignored. In reaction to this trend, I became the founder (and only member) of an organization named Tune's Rights to make sure that the tune gets equal consideration. Both text and tune must have their own integrity and then graciously accommodate one another.

HYFRYDOL hymn texts from three centuries (Figure 8.2–p. 76):

> Come, thou long expected Jesus,
> Born to set thy people free;
> From our fears and sins release us,
> Let us find our rest in thee.
> Israel's strength and consolation,
> Hope of all the earth thou art;
> Dear desire of ev'ry nation,
> Joy of ev'ry longing heart.
> —Charles Wesley, 1707–1788

Alleluia! Sing to Jesus,
His the scepter, his the throne;
Alleluia! His the triumph,
His the victory alone;
Hark! The songs of peaceful Zion
Thunder like a mighty flood;
Jesus out of ev'ry nation
Hath redeemed us by his blood.

—William C. Dix, 1837–1898

Not to us be glory given
But to him who reigns above;
Glory to the God of heaven
For his faithfulness and love!
What though unbelieving voices
Hear no word and see no sign,
Still in God my heart rejoices,
Working out his will divine.

—Timothy Dudley-Smith, b. 1926,
Copyright © 1984 Hope Publishing Company, Carol
Stream, IL 60188. Used by permission.

— REFLECTIONS —

Text and tune:

Look at some of the songs in this book with the following questions in mind:

- What is the mood/voice of the text? Of the tune? Do they match (e.g., both sad) or contrast? If contrasting, can you name the two qualities?
- Where is the climax of the text? Of the tune? Do they match? If not, does it help or hinder the whole?
- Mark the loaded syllables in the text. Does the tune allow them to speak?
- Mark the throwaway syllables in the text. Does the tune also treat them lightly? Or does it place them on strong or long beats?
- Look at subsequent verses. Do they fit? Does it matter?

  Is there a place that really doesn't fit? (Sing it aloud to test it.)

  Is it due to the text? The translation? The tune? The version of the tune?

  Can you find a way to fix it with slight changes? What and where?

- Is there a difference between tunes that start on the downbeat and those that don't?
- Is there a difference between tunes in duple meter and those in triple?
- What is the difference between metric and free pieces? What happens to the text when you try first one, then the other?
- Can you find a song *not* in the book that is a fine example of a good match? Look in a folksong collection, a hymnal, or in popular songs.
- Can you find a bad match? What is wrong?

Extra verses for "My Bonnie" (Figure 8.4—p. 78):

O blow ye winds over the ocean,
And blow ye winds over the sea,
O blow ye winds over the ocean,
And bring back my Bonnie to me.

Last night as I lay on my pillow,
Last night as I lay on my bed,
Last night as I lay on my pillow,
I dreamt that my Bonnie was dead.

MELODIC STYLES

CHAPTER 9:
IN HISTORY

IF WE USE a hymnal as the sourcebook for examining historical changes in tunes, we can see the development in microcosm. The examples are brief, dated, and comprehensible. The fact that they are often much edited and given inauthentic settings can be overcome if we keep several pertinent questions in mind as we look at the melody alone, not the setting.

- When was this first sung? Where? In what language?
- What was its original function?
- Who first notated it? When? Where? Can you visualize such a page?
- Who actually made these marks on this page?
- How many layers is this from the original? Is this a dependable source?

The aim of this brief survey is to trace the shifts in melodic thinking in the Western tradition through notated sacred song. Hymnals give us dates and origins of many melodies, so they are helpful in exploring history. If the melody was originally a folk tune, it will undoubtedly have a country or region of origin; these songs will be discussed in the next chapter.

MEDIEVAL

Our earliest notated examples are from the chant tradition, defined as a song based on the rhythms of spoken language. Chant reflects the subtlety of human speech, which constantly varies in duration, accent, phrase length, and expressive articulation. It is impossible to notate in our present system, which is founded on ratios. The flowing calligraphy of Gregorian notation is much clearer, for we see the pitch markings (the neumes) flying and clustering like birds above the text.

FIGURE 9.1. "Kyrie" from *Missa Orbis*

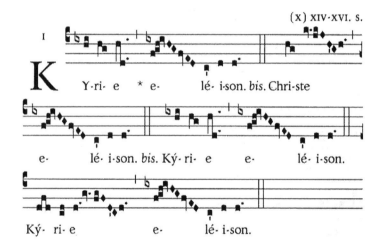

For many people today the notion of "free" or speech rhythm in music is difficult. We are so used to harnessing words into beats that it's hard to undo that bond. But we must make the attempt because only then can the subtle beauties of the single-line melody be released. When we get it right, when the words are enhanced by the curling melodic phrases, it is an unparalleled path to contemplation, to mystical ecstasy. One must listen so completely to other singers, one must so submerge the ego in these rigorous demands, so focus on the sound and meaning of the text, that all else disappears. Because there is no hurry, we can relax. Because the voice is never pushed, we can sing beautifully. Because we are so completely immersed in the text, its meaning is revealed to us in full glory. This music is the perfect antidote to the tension, hurry, and loudness of our times.

The existence of unmetered music gives us another fundamental question to ask a tune: are you free or metered? (I often use the terms "pitch piece" and "rhythm piece" to denote these two extremes.) We must read the page completely differently in each case. Modern notation works *against* the pitch piece and *for* the metric one. All our tunes are notated in ratios, but don't assume that the melody has to have a beat. Try different possibilities: is it possible to sing this tune in chant style? (Remember "Oh, Shenandoah"?) Read the text beautifully, and see if you can keep that same declamation as you add the pitches. If it works, you have made a valuable discovery. These free melodies are rare and give us a chance to use our voices (and appreciate the text) in a very different way. (Try the melodies of "O Come, O Come Emanuel" or "O Sacred Head, Now Wounded.")

RENAISSANCE

When we add metered rhythm to the medieval chant, we get the music of the Renaissance. The tunes dating from ca. 1500–ca. 1650 are all dances or madrigals; they invite the participation of the body. There are modes for the rhythms added to those of the pitches, and most possibilities were delightfully explored. Figure 9.2 provides an example of Renaissance writing.

FIGURE 9.2. "Men G'müt ist mir verwirret"

Mein G'müt ist mir ver-wir-ret, das macht ein Jungk-frau Zart;
bin gantz und gar ver-ir-ret, mein Hertz das kränckt sich hart.

Hab tag und nacht kein ruh, führ all-zeit gro-sse klag,

Thu stets seufftzen und wei-nen, in trau-ren schier ver-zag.

Text and tune: Hans Leo Hassler, 1562–1612
(Translation: My heart is all a-flutter and sick over a sweet lady. There is no rest from my complaining; I am sunk in despair and tears.)

Notation was developing rapidly at this time, along with the invention of the printing press, and this influence spread rapidly. Writing music down stops the music and begins to influence the way we think about it. We begin to cut down on the possibilities open to the listening ear and voice, limiting them to what can be notated. Thus, as notation developed, melodies tended to become less complex. (Think of the difficulties of using Western musical notation for traditional Asian or Middle Eastern song.)

BAROQUE

Harmony develops quickly in the Baroque period (ca. 1650–ca. 1720). Melodies become more and more simplified to accommodate the increasingly complex harmonic movement beneath, and we see intricate chant melodies that metamorphose into Renaissance dance rhythms and later are reduced to plain quarter notes. The following example is characteristic of Baroque style (Figure 9.3; compare with Figure 9.2).

FIGURE 9.3. Passion Chorale from *St. Matthew Passion*

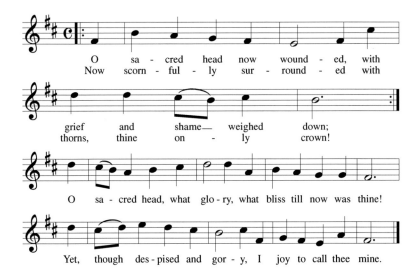

O sa - cred head now wound - ed, with
Now scorn - ful - ly sur - round - ed with

grief and shame— weighed down;
thorns, thine on - ly crown!

O sa - cred head, what glo - ry, what bliss till now was thine!

Yet, though des - pised and gor - y, I joy to call thee mine.

Text and tune: J. S. Bach

CLASSICAL

In Western European music, it's almost as if the process for 400 years was one of increasing melodic simplification, cresting in the Classical period (ca. 1720–ca. 1800). Here are easier melodies, fewer meters, more limited scales (tonal rather than modal), and an almost childlike simplicity at the core. "Twinkle, Twinkle Little Star" is an apt example. (Mozart wrote variations on this folk tune.) What gives it its charm is the delicate balance within these simplified elements and the elegant expression of subtle emotional states. That balance can't—and didn't—last long.

ROMANTIC

In the Romantic era, the nineteenth century, harmony is king and instruments reign supreme, orchestras and halls get larger, symphonies and tone poems get longer, and a virtuoso mindset heralds the advent of the superstar era. There is not much room here for additions to the hymnal. The few we have from known composers are apt to be themes adapted from instrumental works, as is the example in Figure 9.4.

FIGURE 9.4. Robert Schumann's *Nachtstück*, Op. 23, No. 4

Lord, speak to me that I may speak
In living echoes of thy tone;
As thou hast sought, so let me seek
Thine erring children, lost and lone.
                    —Frances Ridley Havergal, 1836–1879

But folk songs continue to be used in instrumental works, adding to the national character of such pieces as Brahms's *Academic Festival Overture*. On the other hand, there are many composers who write only hymns or "parlor" songs: P. P. Bliss, W. B. Bradbury, Fanny Crosby, I. D. Sankey, W. H. Doane, etc. They and others wrote music or words or both using the familiar musical language of the day in much imitated patterns.

TWENTIETH CENTURY

Then comes the twentieth century (we can no longer call it contemporary music) and the collapse of traditional harmonies, and the springing up of various alternative systems. Along with this we find the increasing importance of the page. Notation, interpreted more and more strictly, provides a basis for resisting the overblown Romantic style. Improvisation, melody, and informal music-making all take refuge in the rapidly developing jazz forms. Again, the well-known composers of the day did not concern themselves with small forms like hymns—with one giant exception. Ralph Vaughan Williams used all his skill as a composer and folklorist not only to add magnificent new hymns to the canon, but even to edit *The English Hymnal 1906*, which broke new ground in its respect for past styles and the inclusion of genuine folk melodies.

FIGURE 9.5. "For All the Saints"

For all the saints, who from their la - bors rest, who

thee by faith be - fore the world con - fessed, thy

name, O Je - sus, be for - ev - er__ bless'd, al -

le - lu - ia, al - le - lu - ia.

Text: William W. How, 1823–1897
Tune: Ralph Vaughan Williams, 1872–1958

It is the gradual acceptance of world music that distinguishes hymnals of the twentieth century: first British, then carols from European countries, then, at mid-century, a rush of spirituals as well as Hispanic, Asian, and African songs. We are now, in many Christian denominations, exuberantly multicultural, discovering that loved melodies in one society can transfer wonderfully—with careful translations and editing—to another.

Now, in the new millennium we discover that melody is not dead, that triadic harmonies may be out of fashion in the academy but flourish in popular music, that mothers still sing to their babies, children still sing jump rope games, and love songs are as tonal as ever. We surely don't sing at work as people once did (a room full of computer keyboards is hardly conducive to song). But we are living in a wonderful moment when a wide spectrum of styles is open to the composer and performer, and the greedy listener can happily drown in an ocean of CDs and concert performances. All this is reflected in our hymnals from the contemporary Christian folk song to the intricacies of African rhythms and Oriental nuance.

— REFLECTIONS —

History:

- Begin to cultivate your sense of musical styles in history. Explore a hymnal, learning to ignore the harmonies, listening to how the melody sounds by itself. Sing it exactly as it is written, and then try some experiments.
- Ask the tune some questions:

  Can you be sung in free rhythms?

  Are you a madrigal?

  Could you have been written by Mozart? Brahms?
- Is it possible that this tune has been squeezed into a regular meter? Is there too little or too much time at phrase endings? Do different verses want different rhythms? (Sometimes a negative answer is helpful: you have begun to hear what the tune is *not*.)
- Try the same exercise with a folksong collection with some different questions.

  What was the original function of this song? Work, play, dance, love, grieving, remembering?

  Who might have sung it the first time? Woman, man, child, elder?

  Where? Indoors, outside, in a concert hall, in a living room?

  Why? What has just happened to make this song inevitable?

The aim is to escape the precision of the page and allow the song to "sound" in the voice. Be careful to respect composed tunes—but also look for older editions that might be closer to the composer's intentions. Be free with folk songs. What might have been the original-language text for this tune? Be very sensitive to the limitations of notation. The music is in the air.

CHAPTER 10:
IN GEOGRAPHY

LANGUAGE IS, of course, the great geographical boundary in folk song: think of the different ways that French and German feel in the mouth, and multiply that by an exponential number of native tongues. But each living language poses another conundrum: Where exactly is this song from? Or this singer? There is almost as great a difference between Oxbridge English and an Alabama drawl as between Swedish and Hindi. Let me posit a few rules:

1) Any folk song sounds best in its original language. (Translations may be familiar and much loved, but cannot substitute for the original.) A good, singable translation is rare.

2) Within any language there are regional idioms: these are of prime importance. (This is not so much to identify the original as to select just the right version for your particular use.)

3) In singing, the way vowels and consonants vibrate in the voice box is almost more important than the meaning of the text. (That's a tough one—but there seems to be at this time a general misconception that if the words express a clear thought or emotion, it doesn't matter what the specific words are or how they are pronounced. Test this on spirituals.)

4) Large or small variations in tune or text are characteristic of folk songs. (Again, the operative principle is choice. Which version do you prefer for this performance, here, now?)

5) *Any* notation distorts the song. (No system of notation can account for the myriad subtle variations in any one performance.)

6) Context (costume, dance, traditional instruments, etc.) can be helpful in determining performance style.

Ethnomusicologists, folklore specialists, and students of language divide the globe in many illuminating ways to illustrate families of belief or practice. In this brief study I use only the most general regions, and those were selected because of the specific example I've chosen to cite: European, Southeastern European—Northern Mediterranean, African, Asian, Latin American, and North American (which is in itself a compendium of all the others).

EUROPEAN

European folk song is characterized by its closeness to high culture, musically speaking. The modal, free, improvisatory melodies are generally older than those conforming to a tonal, harmonic pattern. (But all generalizations are dangerous.) Within the British Isles there are at least four major divisions, corresponding roughly to regional boundaries: English, Welsh, Scottish, and Irish. But the Celtic tradition exists in a broad swath from northwestern France through all four countries above, which share a very distinctive common pattern exemplified in the haunting modal curves and repeated words in this mountain ballad.

FIGURE 10.1. "The Chickens They Are Crowing"

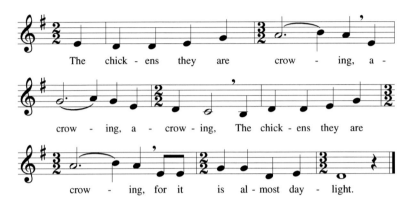

The chick - ens they are crow - ing, a -
crow - ing, a - crow - ing, The chick - ens they are
crow - ing, for it is al - most day - light.

Text and tune: English and Appalachian folk song

This Spanish love song sounds very different with its linked verses, its centering on the third of the scale, and its three-measure phrases (Figure 10.2).

FIGURE 10.2. "Al Olivo"

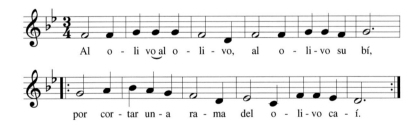

Al o - li vo al o - li - vo, al o - li - vo su bí,
por cor - tar un - a ra - ma del o - li - vo ca - í.

Text and tune: Spanish traditional

(Translation of all verses: From the olive tree I fell. Who helped me rise? A dark-eyed maiden, who gave me her hand. She's the one I love, who must become my wife.)

SOUTHEASTERN EUROPEAN—NORTHERN MEDITERRANEAN

It is revealing that I have no examples from this region. Is it that the Arabic language does not translate easily to our culture? Or that the vocal style, with quarter tones and pitch slides, resists our notation? Certainly I hear much that I find fascinating on the radio—but how much of this is traditional, how much a "mixed" style? These next two songs show a bit of an Eastern influence.

The Magyars lived on the plains of Eastern Europe; many of their songs have characteristic scale patterns and changing meters. This text in Figure 10.3 is in Hungarian.

FIGURE 10.3. "Császárkörte nem vadalma"

Text and tune: Magyar traditional

(This is the old story of a soldier who does not return to his waiting "true love.")

The intense melancholy of the Spanish Jews, persecuted from every side, is evident in the following deeply felt lullaby (Figure 10.4).

FIGURE 10.4. "Durme, Durme"

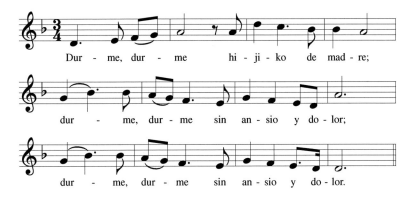

Dur - me, dur - me hi - ji - ko de mad - re;

dur - me, dur - me sin an - sio y do - lor;

dur - me, dur - me sin an - sio y do - lor.

Text and tune: Ladino traditional

(Translation: Sleep, my little son, far from worry and grief. Hear your mother's words: *Shema Yisrael.* Sleep in the beauty of *Shema Yisrael.*)

AFRICAN

A highly developed complexity of rhythmic patterns has evolved from an aural tradition rich in virtuoso techniques. Hundreds of languages and tribal customs yield an astonishing variety of forms and sounds, from storytelling to dance. The listener is almost always involved in refrains and in movements. Dance, theatre, myth, religion, poetry, narrative—all the arts combine. What would it have been like before the European incursions? We can't know—but would there have been the constant use of harmonic thirds (as in Ladysmith Black Mombazo)? I tend to doubt that, going on the examples of African American spirituals, but there is no way of proving it. See Figure 10.5 for one example of a tune from Ghana.

FIGURE 10.5. CHEREPONI

Je - su,—— Je - su,—— fill us with your love, show

us how to serve the neigh - bors we have from you.——

Kneels at the feet of his friends, si - lent - ly wash - es their

feet, mas - ter who acts as a slave—— to them.——

Text: Tom Colvin, 1969
Tune: Ghanaian folk song; arr. Tom Colvin, 1969. Copyright © 1969 Hope Publishing
Company, Carol Stream, IL 60188. Used by permission.

ASIAN

I have slight knowledge of Asian folk music but must use my intuition because the songs are there, waiting to be interpreted. Those examples I know appear in hymnals, where the translations are often totally inadequate. If the writer is fluent neither in English nor in our form of musical notation, one must often intuit what the song may have sounded like in finding a version of the song that truly communicates to Western listeners. The addition of Western harmonies is almost always fatal. The challenge is to remember the voices from the country that one has heard in travel or on recordings and to try to reproduce the vocal quality and the affect of the song. It should sound different from American songs. Lean on the differences. Does it have a nasal vocal quality? Is there a quaver in the voice? Imagine singers in native dress accompanied by traditional instruments. How does this affect the sounds you make?

This Filipino hymn moves in a serene calm. Figure 10.6 shows how it appears in current hymnals; Figure 10.7 is my version, reflecting an unhurried, chant-like reflection of the word rhythms.

FIGURE 10.6. "Wasdin"

Text and tune: F. F. Feliciano, copyright © 1983 Abingdon Press, *Hymns from the Four Winds*

FIGURE 10.7. "Wasdin"—renotated

Text and tune: F. F. Feliciano, copyright © 1983 Abingdon Press, *Hymns from the Four Winds*

This twelfth-century Japanese song is unbelievably atmospheric, different from any other songs I know in its low first phrase and keening high notes in the middle (Figure 10.8).

FIGURE 10.8. "Imayo"

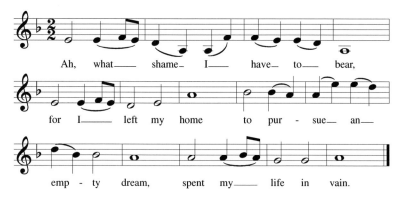

Ah, what— shame— I— have— to— bear,

for I— left my home to pur - sue— an—

emp - ty dream, spent my— life in vain.

Text: tr. E. Hibbard, from *Cantate Domino: An Ecumenical Hymn Book*. Original Japanese text: Sogo Matsumoto © Church of Christ, Tokyo. Tune: 12th c. Japanese

LATIN AMERICAN

I have visited both Argentina and Venezuela and have been delighted with the vitality of their singing traditions. Publishing is expensive and relatively rare, so learning by ear is a much stronger factor, with the consequent ease in improvisation and the assimilation of new tunes. It's rather hard to define "folk song" here because it doesn't carry the divisive connotation that it does in North America. Traditional and newly composed songs coexist in happy confusion. Many new songs are instantly adopted into the folk canon, and it can be difficult to find out who composed a particular song or whether, indeed, it has a composer. This hymn from Argentina has a characteristically lively rhythm and a hard-to-forget refrain (Figure 10.9).

FIGURE 10.9. "Canto de Esperanza"

Text: Alvin Schutmaat copyright © 1984 *Presbyterian Mission Yearbook for Prayer and Study*
Tune: ARGENTINA, Argentine folk melody

(Translation: God of Hope, give us joy and peace! To a world in crisis, speak your truth. God of Justice, show us your light—light and hope in the darkness. We pray for peace; we sing of your love; we work for peace, faithful to you, Lord.)

NORTH AMERICAN

People brought their songs to Canada and the U.S. as they colonized the land, so we have examples from all around the world as our polyglot inheritance. There are many examples elsewhere in this book. Native Americans provide the closest true examples of resident folk music, yet I find the language and melodic patterns so foreign to my tradition that I can only listen and admire. The tunes do not become part of my vocabulary, but the texts in various translations are wonderfully evocative. Canada boasts a lively French-speaking culture, faintly echoed in the New Orleans area (itself brightly flavored by the surrounding African American influence).

African American spirituals are to my knowledge the only folk form developed in the United States, but what a form that is. It is a hybrid, springing from the collision of African languages and songs with the Western European hymns and folk dances the slaves heard on the plantations. Born in suffering, the chief artistic outlet open to a profoundly creative people, the slave songs encapsulate human emotion in melodies that range from soaring flow to playful patter. Because no notation was involved in their transmission, they are pure examples of the oral tradition at work, with many variations and different settings of similar texts and with subtle play on pitches and rhythms. Because tune and text evolved together, there is never a discontinuity. Developed from the sixteenth to the nineteenth centuries from New England to the deep south, the central canon reflects the unquenchable spirit of a people who should have been without hope, but who were able to affirm even their suffering. I think it is this quality that makes spirituals speak so strongly to people everywhere. We all share in that affirmation.

"Deep River" has an almost iconic presence in our collective memories (Figure 10.10). I like to think of it as having a chant-like freedom in the refrain and then a more rhythmic verse. In contrast, "I Got a Key to thuh Kingdom" exemplifies the fast patter-song that pulses with rhythmic energy reflecting the zeal of the singer (Figure 10.11).

FIGURE 10.10. "Deep River"

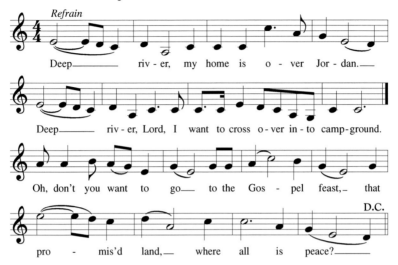

Text and tune: African American spiritual

FIGURE 10.11. "I Got a Key to thuh Kingdom"

Text and tune: African American spiritual

Since the spread around the globe of television, CDs, and music videos, it has become more and more difficult to hear native cultures not influenced by the sounds emanating from the American music industry. The popular music scene is not folk music by any definition, yet it is founded upon strong regional styles coming from Western Europe (tonality and simple harmonies), Africa (complex rhythms, call-and-response patterns, much repetition), and Latino strains (dances involving cross-rhythms and intricate tune-text relationships). And the more the electronic culture spreads, the more it brings back to us examples from groups and individuals we've never heard before, with seemingly inexhaustible new ways of combining words and notes. What it will develop into is impossible to foretell. It seems now that the commercial/consumer proliferation of music has badly eroded the way actual human beings have always developed and transmitted song. But I refuse to be discouraged; the true voices are there, if momentarily overwhelmed. It is a fascinating time to be alive and singing, cherishing both the pure melodies that come to us from times past and the new tunes that begin to herald the onset of a one-world musical language.

— REFLECTIONS —

In geography:

• Begin your own collection of folk songs from different cultures.
• Can you find examples of different scales? Rhythms? Dances? Functions?
• Can you verbalize their characteristic traits?

More verses for "The Chickens They Are Crowing"
(Figure 10.1—p. 99):

My mother she will scold me, scold me, scold me,
My mother she will scold me for staying away all night.

My father, he'll uphold me, uphold me, uphold me,
My father, he'll uphold me and say I've done just right.

I won't go home till morning, till morning, till morning,
I won't go home till morning, and I'll stay with the girls all night.

More verses for "Al Olivo" (Figure 10.2—p. 99):

Del olivo cai, ¿Quien me levantara?
Una gachi morena, Que la mano me da. (2x)

Que la mano me da, Que la mano me dió,
Esa gachi morena Es la que quiero yo. (2x)

Es la que quiero yo, Es la que he de querer,
Esa gachi morena Ha de ser mi mujer. (2x)

More verses for "Durme, Durme" (Figure 10.4—p. 104):

Siente joya palavrikas de tu Madre,
Las palavras di Shema Yisrael. (2x)

Durme, durme hijiko de Madre,
Con hermozura Di Shema Yisrael. (2x)

More verses for "Wasdin" (Figure 10.6—p. 103):

Come, listen to the trees,
The green fields, the rivers, and the morning breeze,
The birds of the air all singing their Maker's praise.
Creator of countless wonders,
Who else could it be?

Yes, I am filled with peace,
For I feel the presence of the Lord my God.
Your praise I will sing, my Maker, Creator of all,
Because when I think of your works,
Joy reigns in my heart.
—F. F. Feliciano, copyright © 1983 Abingdon Press

More verses for "Imayo" (Figure 10.8—p. 104):

In this hut I sleep and wake,
Taking care of swine.
No one has pity on me.
Loud blows the chilly wind.

Tattered sleeves are wet with dew
When I think of home.
Waking from my foolish dreams,
To my home I'll go.

— © World Council of Churches (Ester Hibbard 1962)

CHAPTER 11:
IN FUNCTION

SONGS DO NOT EXIST in a vacuum. They fill needs of specific human beings in specific times and places, and come most alive when the setting is reproduced at least in the imagination. To begin to recover the living articulation of a written melody, ask some questions.

HOW WAS IT USED?

Where does it fit in the human life cycle? If we adapt Shakespeare's seven ages of man, this gives us a framework to see how song relates to each stage. *Infant*: lullaby, play; *child*: games, learning, dance; *young adult*: love, occupations, parenting, diversion; *mature adult*: philosophy, remembering, subtlety; *elder*: disengagement, loss; *ending*: death, elegy, mourning.

The list is by no means definitive, but it serves as a beginning graph for plotting song functions. And there are two great qualities arching across the whole lifespan: remembering and humor. The declaration of love sung by a seventeen-year-old sounds very different from the same song sung by one fifty years older. A work song to unite men hoisting sail sounds very different from the same song transposed in time and space to the concert hall. Sung with humor, a serious love song can turn into a teasing parody or an ironic undercutting of the sentiment expressed in the text.

When I was very young, I was sure that this next example was a sweet love song—until I grew old enough to understand the reference to the "herring boxes without topses" that served as sandals for a not-very-petite Clementine (Figure 11.1). Sing it with a backcountry twang and a twinkle in the eye.

FIGURE 11.1. "Clementine"

In a ca - vern, in a can - yon, ex - ca - va - ting for a
Refrain: Oh my dar - ling, Oh my dar - ling, Oh my dar - ling Cle - men -

mine, dwelt a mi – ner, for - ty - ni - ner and his
tine, you are lost and gone for - e - ver, dread - ful

daugh - ter Cle - men - tine.
sor - ry Cle - men - tine.

Text and tune: Percy Montross, ca. 1880

HOW CAN ONE MOVE TO IT?

Only an overly intellectualized society would think of separating music, words, and dance into different arts. Of course, they can exist independently, but they begin together. Look at any two-year-old, unable to hear music and remain quietly seated. Think of the primacy of dance in preliterate societies. Eric Havelock, in *The Muse Learns to Write*, comments on the meaning of the Greek work *mousike*: "As you recited you sang, as you sang you played an instrument, as you played you danced, these motions being performed collectively. Their unusually sophisticated partnership supplied mutual reinforcement." This was needed for the recitation of lengthy genealogies, histories, or stories in ancient Greece and in other cultures.

One does not need a background in dance studies to imagine the possible movement of the human body to different kinds of melody. Think arms, legs, trunk, head. Think balance, self-contained or outward reaching. Think motion across the floor, fast or slow. Think motion up and down, abrupt or smooth, long-line or short, interrupted patterns. Think humorous or serious, dainty or rough, tender or scornful. Imagine different people moving to the same strains. Realize that all musical rhythm—even free, unmeasured rhythms—finds its source in movements of the human body. (A clock, metronome, or drum machine is not a musical instrument.)

IS ITS PRIMARY FUNCTION TO UNITE A GROUP?

Work songs certainly fall in this category, as do many dances and play-party songs. In worship, chants and hymns unite congregations in most of the world's religions. As part of a ceremony (as in military, court, or ecclesiastical festivities), music is a mighty unifier (think of Sousa marches).

But what happens when the function seems not only to unite but to manipulate the singers and listeners? About music used as propaganda or distraction, the theologian Dorothy Sayers writes in *The Whimsical Christian*: "Let us take the amusement art. What we demand from it is the enjoyment of the emotions that usually accompany experience without having had the experience...Or take the spellbinding kind of art...This pseudoart seeks to produce the behavior without the experience. In its vulgarest form it becomes pure propaganda. It can actually succeed in making its audience into the thing it desires to have them [be]...This pseudoart does not really communicate power to us; it merely exerts power over us."

This leads us to a last, very subtle function, that of the communication of power. My belief is that long-lasting, true melodies do exactly this. They do it in the church, the theatre, and the home. They do it for the individual as well as the group. Look at the uses of music in our society, the enormous influence of the different branches of popular music, including the recording industry; the advertising jingle; the world of drama, including cinema, musical comedy, and opera; the classical concert; and academia. Notice in how many of these the possibility of the empowerment of the individual has been subverted by the combination of advertising and electronics. The chance of a song's finding its own level by slow spreading from group to group is gone. Now popular music is engineered by people in the entertainment industry, and sales are the arbiter of success. (Hence the enormous sums earned by the writers of often-played commercials.)

At the other end of the power spectrum is great religious music. Here the texts deal with the great mysteries of life; the music to which they are set, exactly because of its non-specific nature, is uniquely qualified to illumine these ponderings on the meaning of life, on love and loss, on suffering and transcendence. Through time and tone it is possible to construct an architecture of order, a glimpse of an ideal world. We can be transformed by adapting our thoughts to these eternal physical realities, which help us to overcome our very real limitations. This is empowerment indeed: great truths of physical energy plus imaginative vision plus human consolation are experienced through great music. Here is the highest function of music-making. In the words of Abraham Joshua Heschel: "Listening to great music is a shattering experience, throwing the soul into an encounter with an aspect of reality to which the mind can never relate itself adequately...I spend my life working with thoughts. And one problem that gives me no rest is: Do these thoughts ever rise to the heights reached by authentic music?"

— REFLECTIONS —

In function:

- How many functions for songs can you list?
- What are the functions of advertising jingles? Marches? Pop song ballads? Old ballads? Lonesome tunes? Dance tunes? (name the dance)
- What different qualities must they have to accomplish their function?

More verses to "Clementine" (Figure 11.1—p. 114):

Light she was and like a fairy, and her shoes were number nine,
Herring boxes without topses sandals were for Clementine.
Refrain

Drove she ducklings to the water every morning just at nine,
Stubbed her toe upon a splinter, fell into the foaming brine.
Refrain

Ruby lips above the water blowing bubbles soft and fine;
Alas for me, I was no swimmer, so I lost my Clementine.
Refrain

In a churchyard near the canyon where the myrtle doth entwine
Grow the rosies and other posies, fertilized by Clementine.
Refrain

THE NEW ELEMENT

CHAPTER 12:
FUNDAMENTAL ENERGY

W HEN RHYTHM, pitch, and word combine in just the right propor-
tions, an organism like a living form results. This form is balanced
within and cohesive without, pulsing with life. It is one whole with a
beginning, middle, and end. It sets up an expectation and fulfills it. It
is capable of reproduction; it bears repetition and endless variation. It
fulfills its function. It seems inevitable. It lasts.

Melodies that endure are like fundamental physical forms:
cloud, stream, tree. They have a rightness in which each element
is subordinate to the whole and everything works together for
structural unity. Tiny cells (the individual duration + pitch + syllable)
grow into larger units (one tune = one cloud). This tune itself is
expandable through strophic forms in which the same melody adapts
to different words or through a free extension into the variation,
contrast, and great tension of, say, sonata form.

What makes these durable tunes different from other thousands
composed during the same time period? It's this rightness, this
complexity-within-simplicity, this balancing of elements that
is impossible to categorize, to reduce to a set of rules, yet easy to
recognize in the immense satisfaction that it gives in performance.
Why are we so enamored of them that we sing them over and over? I
think it is because both they and we are aligned with fundamental
physical matter. Both of us are part of the universe, and we vibrate

together in the performance. (This is as true of a slow, sad song as of a lively one.) The singing literally energizes us, like a jolt of some divine elixir that helps us to drop off the cares of everyday life and remember who and where we really are.

This process is as true for the composer as for the performer. Whether we are creating or recreating, each one of us works in his or her individual way. No one can give us any infallible rules about how to do it. Writing a tune is, I believe, more a mysterious process of allowing it to flow through one (*a la* Mozart, Schubert, and Gershwin) than a laborious construction (although this is possible: see the choral hymn from Beethoven's Ninth Symphony). Each of those creators, as well as the anonymous first singer of a spiritual, is in alignment with the created world, and guides the phrase into a channel carved by and into eternity. The wonder is that so many combinations are possible, like the stars in the sky or the sands on the shore. Of course, there are echoes of other combinations, but if the "floating phrase" of text or tune is integrated into this particular whole, then it is right.

The issue here is not originality but inevitability. Our society's preoccupation with originality has been one of the great misapprehensions of these times. Novelty is certainly a welcome component in art, but surely not the *sine qua non* of artistic achievement. Pushing back the boundaries is often the role of the young and the reckless, but profundity more often seems to look inward rather than out. The greatest art can arise from the simplest and most timeworn materials.

Another precept that we learn from physics is that of opposing forces: matter and anti-matter, positive and negative. What opposing energies surround this lasting tune (Figure 12.1)?

FIGURE 12.1. "L'amour de moy"

Text and tune: French 16th c.

(Translation: My love is hidden within a charming garden, where roses and lilies grow, and hollyhocks. This garden is sweet and gay, filled with all flowers. One may there find pleasure by night and day.)

THE ANATOMY OF MELODY — ALICE PARKER

Think of it as a flower that you wish to display in the most perfect setting. The vase, the table, the backdrop, the light—all contribute to the whole, and offer a different aspect with each different angle of vision. The tune is the flower. Once I have plucked it out of the flow of improvisatory song, I must decide how to display it.

No two people will sing it the same way. The test of success or failure is, I believe, energy. Are the forces here recreated in such a way as to transmit that balance of the whole? Or are they dissipated in details like diction, tone production, or correctness-to-the-page? If just one person is singing, the song fits the lips and can fill a hall. But if two or more join together, we get a different scenario. For now variation is present. There is no way that two people can sing and sound like one. The more people involved, the more variation is possible. Imagine an improvisatory session with, say, the Preservation Hall Jazz Band. How would they sound if they played the same melody in unison? Would they strive for perfect tuning and balance? Or would they take more delight in the different versions and tone colors sounding at the same time?

The tune in Figure 12.2 is well known to all the performers of the Preservation Hall Jazz Band. Its aura and its surrounding energies are the implied harmonies and countermelodies contained within its single line. In a five-minute performance I heard several years ago, the players were all riding these implications at the same time, playing games with these very simple words (only this one verse) and notes. They explored differing and complementary possibilities of statement and answer, solo and chorus, complexity and simplicity, tension and release, climax and resolution. It's a cosmic game of energy: if they ride together, the game continues. If one drops the ball, the game may falter momentarily or even collapse, often in laughter. But then it starts again—*each time different.* While there may be "floating phrases" that recur, there is no attempt to replicate exactly the previous moves.

124

FIGURE 12.2. "Put on Your Old Grey Bonnet"

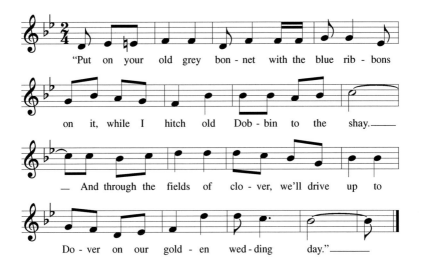

Text: Stanley Murphy, 1909
Tune: Percy Weinrich, 1909

(That would be like a basketball game in which the players are asked to duplicate precisely the steps that led to a previous victory. It can't be done. There are too many conflicting details. If you're concentrating on where to put your foot, you miss the ball. So you learn to savor the game rather than the result, the process rather than the product.) And the product (back to music) may sound very inadequate on a recording, but that does not at all reflect the pleasure that the players and listeners have enjoyed at the actual game.

James P. Carse, in his book *Finite and Infinite Games*, discourses wonderfully on this principle of gamesmanship. Where traditional scoring posits a win-lose situation, the open-ended game exists *in order to continue.* Learning to look at music in this way requires practice and the suspension of some of our cherished beliefs about perfection in performance. In this way of looking, perfection itself is the keeping-going, the continual inviting into the game of new players, and of valuing all the varied viewpoints. The idea is not to do *the* perfect performance, but to keep the melody alive, the song singing, and the energy refreshing to everyone within hearing. And when we have to stop—the song is there, ready to be picked up the next time.

This kind of music-making is transformative. It should be just as much in tune, in time, and in style as we can make it, but it's much more than that. It is merging with the creative energies that propel the universe, absorbing us all into the stream of life.

— REFLECTIONS —

Fundamental energy: "L'amour de moy" (Figure 12.1):

- Analyze the tune and text for phrase curves, structure, repetition, mood, and more.
- Find other examples of energy in nature (a tree, a flower, a cloud, water, microphotographs of natural processes).
- In the visual arts, notice how Van Gogh treats trees, wind, and sky in his paintings.
- Trace the curves of the animals painted on the caves at Lascaux and the interrelationship of pattern and color in Indonesian batiks.
- Energy and form are all around us. What can you see right now, or hear, or touch, or taste and smell that awakens your understanding?

More verses to "L'amour de moy"—p. 123:

Hélas! Il n'est si doulce chose
Que de ce coulx roussignolet,
Que chante au soir au matinet:
Quand il est las il se repose.

Je la vy l'autre jour cueillir
La violette en ung verd pré,
La plus belle qu'onceques je veis,
Et la plus plaisante à mon gré.

(Translation: Alas! There is no sound so sweet as that of the nightingale who sings from dusk to dawn: when he is tired, he rests. I saw her the other day, gathering violets in a green meadow: the most beautiful sight of all and the most pleasing to me.)

CHAPTER 13:
FORM AND FORMS

IN CHAPTER 7, the explosive combination of pitch elements and rhythmic elements into melody were mentioned. The basic unit of melody is phrase, which is defined by breath. A phrase is what we breathe at the end of. One phrase (of whatever length) equals one breath. One phrase sets up a musical structure that is extended by the next, whether in response or repetition. The larger structure grows organically from the seed. Each song is as different as each plant. There are similar varieties, of course, but at close analysis, each one is unique. The only certainty is that each develops out of its own beginning.

What makes a form successful? For me, the first necessity is inevitability: no bumps, no parts too short or too long, no interruptions to the flow. It has three interlocking sections: beginning, middle, and end. It accomplishes its purpose: dance, mourning, game, lullaby. It fulfills the expectations set up by its first notes. These concepts can be applied to the first phrase as well as to the whole because one is the microcosm of the other. Analyzing the first phrase for its building blocks, its exact components, should be a secure guide to what is to come, both for its content and for what is not there (its opposites).

In Figure 13.1 the text pattern is *ab ab cb db*. The musical pattern is AB A'B' CB C''B'. The refrain contributes two strong elements to the form: unchanging repetition at the end of each line (a small refrain) and the fact that the first two complete lines form another larger refrain. The form unfolds like a flower bud, curving around itself. The call-and-response pattern makes for easy remembering and performing. There are many songs that follow this pattern, but few are as moving and inevitable.

FIGURE 13.1. "Swing Low, Sweet Chariot"

Text and tune: African American spiritual

Basically, musical form is like any other natural structure: a tree, flowing from seed to crown, from root to trunk to twigs. Or a river, growing from streamlet to river to torrent to ocean: each detail is merged into the whole, and no matter what happens (flood or drought) it fulfills natural laws. Learning to listen to where the music wants to go is a large part of creating working structures. The composer or performer may have ideas, but the immediate necessity is to work with the materials at hand, as a carpenter respects the particular piece of wood he or she is shaping.

Musical forms are created structures that we attempt to classify (e.g., by order or genus). They are based on repetition and contrast. Can you imagine listening to music in which each phrase introduces new ideas without hearkening back to an earlier thought? The brain would give up trying to order the flow: the result is either confusion or apathy. Only repetition can give the ear the security it needs to recognize the pattern (think of a remembered face). Variation and thematic development are extensions of repetition: one or more elements of the original idea undergo a change that refreshes the ear. Look at this partial list of elements, which may vary either singly or in different combinations:

pitch	quality of beat
home	*text*
scale/mode	*voicing*
timbre	*articulation*
sonority	*dynamics*
rhythm	*motives*
pulse/meter	*mood/function*
tempo	

The more complex the material, the more repetition is needed. Remembered signposts provide aural recognition. Some are obvious, and others are hidden.

Imagine time as a yardstick. It is analogous to creating a design in space by unifying elements that recur in constantly shifting patterns. This is a fundamental organizing principle in all the arts, but it feels different in the sound world of music. Isaac Watts makes the concept clear in an old hymn.

> Teach me the measure of my days, thou maker of my frame;
> I would survey life's narrow space, and learn how frail I am.
> A span is all that we can boast, an inch or two of time;
> Man is but vanity and dust in all his flower and prime. (see Figure 13.4)

I love the phrase "an inch or two of time." It's helpful to have this visual image of music's time-bound flow.

Again, this concept can be applied to both small and large forms. For a simple song, one verse is the "small form"; the entire song is the "large form"; both need careful structuring in conception and in performance. The two are closely linked. Where the original structure is weak, even the most experienced performer has difficulty projecting a unified whole. But many an unskilled performer has wreaked havoc on a great melody without destroying its essential integrity.

Repetitions can be exact or partial. Think of singing different verses to the same tune. (A mental image may be helpful: picture a screen displaying a graph of the precise sounds reaching its sensors. There's no way we can sing a phrase exactly the same way twice even with the same words.) Contrasts are also exponential in variety. Analyze the characteristics of a melody, and then project the opposite, as in minor/major; *piano/forte*; step/skip; metered/free. Explore these opposites: unity vs. contrast; predictable vs. surprising; simplicity vs. complexity; clear structure vs. uncertainty.

Try singing through these examples. Note the different ways that repetition works within and between the verses. Identify the different materials that unify each song.

FIGURE 13.2. "Guide My Feet"

Text and tune: African American spiritual

FIGURE 13.3. "Death Shall Not Destroy My Comfort"

Text and tune: MT. WATSON, *Wyeth's Repository of Sacred Music*, 1813

Strophic: "The Water Is Wide" (see Figure 8.3)

Song with double refrain: "Swing Low, Sweet Chariot" (see Figure 13.1)

Three-part song: "He's Gone Away" (see Figures 6.4–6.6)

For both composer and interpreter, the question is how to begin. Whence comes the mysterious seed out of which the structure will grow? I remember my fruitless struggles in college trying to write a piece of modern music that couldn't have existed in a previous era. What a dumb idea! Ask a beginner to invent a new genus that shares almost no characteristics with other created structures? There was no listening to a simple idea, only the frustrating standard of negatives: it mustn't be tonal or memorable or easy. This was justified as preparing me for the future. But for me the result was the suppression of my intuitive musical imagination. I grew to distrust my inner voice, and it took years for me to recover it. As I've grown more experienced, it seems that the ability to recognize an idea as a fruitful one is one of the great gifts. The idea itself must be simple (as a seed is simple). Its main function is to grow, to keep providing shoots that lead to new structures.

Years ago I read a wonderful article by Tom Stoppard describing how he starts a new play. A questioner had assumed that he began with a topic in mind, an idea of what it's about. Stoppard wrote something like this: "I wake up one morning with a phrase in my mind—it's being said by someone, a character. I don't know yet who it is. I must write it down and keep writing to discover the character and setting. It's as if I drew a finger on the page—then gradually the hand, the wrist, the forearm—and when I get to the elbow I begin to get an idea of what the picture or the play is about."

That's a clear example of going with the flow, following that first intuitive impulse without analytical or theoretical distractions. In a similar way, a composer may not sit down to write a large formal structure. One follows that first sound in the ear, and what develops from it may be labeled a symphony by someone classifying forms many years later. And one certainly does not sit down to compose "great music" (another of my shibboleths from college). Rather, one follows where one's imagination leads. Of course, what makes a well-constructed piece is technique, the experience of working out many different ideas, and the willingness to critique one's own work. Composition is a craft, just as carpentry or weaving or cooking are crafts. The artist is a craftsperson who has mastered the combination of inspiration with technical prowess.

A closing thought: I learned to teach from a wonderfully strong-minded woman named Helen Crystal Bender. She used to describe adult beginners at the piano with the concise phrase, "Their critical is stronger than their executive," meaning that they were so impatient with their own admittedly feeble achievements that it throttled them from the start. They couldn't just enjoy being where they were and allow skills to develop slowly (is there any other way?) to higher levels. Beginning musicians should learn to value simple ideas and learn to work with them for their many gratifications. Larger forms will follow if the muse leads in that direction. It's pointless to write a song if you can't write a phrase; it's pointless to write an opera if you can't write an aria.

Energy and form are the double helix of creation: they are inseparable. The form is the result of the energies set in motion by the first notes of the song.

—LIST OF ELEMENTS TO CONSIDER IN ANALYZING AND/OR PERFORMING A MELODY—

Voicing: Who is singing?

 solo/group
 high voices/low voices
 old person/young person
 man/woman
 child/grownup

Text: Who is speaking?

 color/idiom
 tone of voice
 meaning
 form (verse structure)
 loaded syllables
 metaphors
 alliteration, etc.

Rhythm: Who is dancing?

 free/metric
 duple/triple
 steady/changing
 fast/slow
 quality of beat (accent, dance)
 tempo

Pitch:

 mode/scale
 home/cadence
 range/tessitura
 sonority
 phrase curves

Articulation:

legato/non-legato

marcato/staccato

Dynamics:

soft/loud

sudden/gradual

Mood/sonority (Can you find the right word?):

swinging

bouncy

firmly

swaying

forceful

with humor

tenderly

teasing

floating, etc.

Form:

phrase structure

question/answer

parallel/opposite

endings/connections

repetition/variation (exact or partial)

beginning/middle/end

climax/resolution

Can you add to this list?

— REFLECTIONS —

Form and forms:

For me, the aim of a formal analysis is to discover the elements of which a song is constructed and to show these in a visual pattern revealing the large structure at one glance. Let me add that the benefit of the analysis is principally in making it, not in the final graph itself.

Any written score is itself a graph of music. But there is so much detail on each page that it's hard to separate the important structural points from the details. Here is a simple graph of "He's Gone Away" (see Figures 6.4–6.6). It allows me to keep the large form in mind while I'm singing.

/ _____ / _____ / _____ / _____

Refrain Verse 1   *Refrain* Verse 2   *Refrain* Verse Recitative   *Refrain* Coda

Another verse for "Swing Low, Sweet Chariot" (Figure 13.1—p. 130):

If you get there before I do,
Comin' for to carry me home.
Tell all my friends that I'm a comin' too.
Comin' for to carry me home.

More verses for "Guide My Feet" (Figure 13.2—p. 133):

Hold my hand…
                    Stand by me…
                              Lead me on…

More verses for "Death Shall Not Destroy My Comfort"
(Figure 13.3—p. 133):

> Jordan's stream shall not o'erflow me
> While my Savior's by my side,
> Canaan, Canaan lies before me,
> Soon I'll cross the swelling tide. *Refrain*

> See the happy spirits waiting
> On the banks beyond the stream;
> Sweet responses still repeating,
> Jesus, Jesus is their theme. *Refrain*

FIGURE 13.4. "Teach Me the Measure" (see p. 132)

Text: Psalm 39, Isaac Watts, *The Psalms of David*, 1719
Tune: SUFFIELD, *Kentucky Harmony*, 1816

More verses for "Teach Me the Measure":

> A span is all that we can boast,
> An inch or two of time;
> Man is but vanity and dust
> In all his flower and prime.

See the vain race of mortals move
Like shadows o'er the plain;
They rage and strive, desire, and love,
But all the noise is vain.

What should I wish or wait for, then,
From creatures, earth and dust?
They make our expectations vain,
And disappoint our trust.

Now I forbid my carnal hope,
My fond desires recall;
I give my mortal int'rest up,
And make my God my all.

—EXAMPLE OF AN ANALYSIS OF FIGURE 13.4, "TEACH ME THE MEASURE"—

Text:

Source: Isaac Watts, Psalm 39 II, 5 vs.

Form: 8.6.8.6

Rhyming: *abab*

Mood: somber meditation on the brevity of life

Voice: formal English

Color words, dynamics, and changing moods:

1) measure, maker, narrow space, frail *mp* sad

2) span, boast, inch, vanity, dust, flower, prime *mf* regret

3) vain, mortals, shadows, rage, strive, desire, love, noise, vain *f* firm

4) wish, wait, creatures, earth, dust, expectations vain, disappoint trust
   pp lost

5) forbid, hope, recall, give up mortal int'rest, my God my all
   mf>p stern, then acceptance

Music:

Source: *Kentucky Harmony*, 1816

Tune: SUFFIELD

Pitches: modal E minor (all seven notes), range D to F-sharp (a tenth), demands good voices

Rhythm: 3–2/2–2, slow, quiet, relentless, coiled energy, half-note pickups, parallel durations 1–3 and 2–4, whole-note endings

Phrases, range, and endings:

1)   gentle curves up and down; fifth, E to B to E;   home

2)   up a third, then stepwise down; fourth, G to B to F-sharp;   away

3)   down from B to E, then dramatic leap up, climax;
     B up again to F-sharp alt, then back to B tenth B to E to F-sharp to B; away

4)   up a second, then stepwise down to E ; sixth, B to C to E;   home

EAR PLAY AND EYE PLAY

CHAPTER 14:
IMPROVISATION

THE PROCESS OF MUSIC-MAKING is often described as a triangle with the composer, performer, and audience at different points. But there is a far more elemental construction that involves only one person who doubles on the spot as composer and performer. In the beginning no outside listener is involved. The delight comes in the sheer joy of playing with the musical materials.

Many small children "own" tunes by changing the words or the rhythm or the notes at their own pleasure, reinventing the song each time they sing it. This is music that exactly suits the moment with no need to become set in a mold. It is endlessly renewable. Adults who are loath to try this freedom should start with the words. Just changing the context of the song can lead to a variation in regional accent, in tempo, or in the quality of the beat. If you slip in an additional syllable, that's the kind of improvising that is almost imperative as you sing the different verses of a ballad. Try this with "Fare Thee Well" (Figure 14.1) on the next page.

Variables include the length of the final note in each phrase; lingering on loaded syllables or high notes; filling in skips; and extending the sung range. Pretend you are a clarinet or trombone, or one or another of your favorite singers. What would they be likely to do with this delightful, brief blues?

Often there are many variations in syllable count from one verse to another, and the good performer or improviser can make these anomalies sound absolutely right, even if it means adding a couple of extra beats to a measure. Ornamenting the pitches of a melody falls into a similar category. I'm always amused at singers who need to have someone write out the ornaments to a Baroque tune for them to learn and then always sing the passage the same way. The name of this game is improvisation, and each performer should be able to make changes that exactly suit his or her instrument and personality at any time and place. The *cadenza* in a concerto is a lengthier form of improvisation that often combines ornamentation with technical acrobatics in variations on the previous themes.

FIGURE 14.1. "Fare Thee Well"

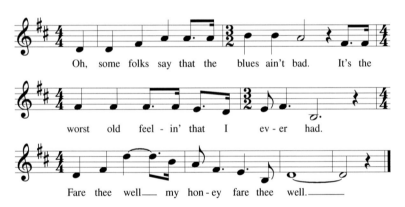

Text and tune: American folk song

If I had wings like Noah's dove,
I'd fly up the river to the one I love: *Refrain*

One of these days an' it won't be long
You'll call my name an' I'll be gone: *Refrain*

In jazz, improvisation is usually based on the harmonic framework of the tune. That is, the chord changes that occur under the melody are repeated in their familiar rhythm, and the soloist is free to create new lines above this foundation, lines that may or may not recall the original melody. (This is a simplistic view of a complex process.) In the best performers, both tune and chord changes are subjected to delightful and surprising transformations.

This is the present version of a very old form, known in previous periods as theme with variations. Typical of the classical period would be a theme presented in very simple rhythms, perhaps quarter notes, which is then expanded into eighth notes, triplets, and sixteenth notes, not to mention going from a major key to its relative minor. When you make this up at the piano, you are improvising. When you write it down, you are composing a theme with variations.

The principal difference is that of making music spontaneously as opposed to learning it from (or writing it on) a page. In this situation, the sense of energy is paramount because there is no time to wait for a good idea or to think ahead to the next entrance. The performer is riding the curve of the line, and success comes (just as it does to the skateboarder) when the energy is triumphantly ridden to its ending. The appeal to the listener is precisely the danger involved. Is the performer daring hugely, and does she succeed? Virtuosity is part of the game, so the better you know your instrument, the more possibilities are open to you. And surprise is another part because it is wonderful to be taken around an unexpected curve.

I often wonder what great improvisers of the past would think of the careful performances we give their works today. Would Mozart ever have played one of his piano concertos exactly the same way? (Think back to the image of the dancer. The choreography is the same, but each night's performance is different, of the moment.) How about Bach on the organ? Or Chopin at the piano? The world of sound was for them a world to leap into and discover just as the diver enters the pool. They would have much more in common with today's jazz virtuosos than with a carefully schooled (and unadventurous) concert artist.

Finally, one of the great satisfactions of improvisatory music-making is that it can't be repeated. It's all or nothing, right here, right now. And it will never be the same again. So it's a lifetime challenge to listen, to respond to that melody, that opportunity, that invitation. If you accept, ride it for all it's worth. It may be exciting and dangerous, but it is surely never boring!

— REFLECTIONS —

Improvisation: "Fare Thee Well" (Figure 14.1):

- How do you set up the rhythm before you begin to sing? Can you imagine the sound of a drum set in your head?
- How long do you hold the end-of-phrase notes? Are they all the same length?
- What is the difference between the verses? Literally, what is the difference in the number of syllables per line? Where do you place the extra ones? Figuratively, what is the mood, tension, climax? Might you change/add notes for emphasis?
- Is the song over when you run out of verses? If not (if there is still energy for continuing), what do you do?
- If you decide to repeat, is it literal or is it different? How? Is there new freedom? To do what?
- How long can you keep it going? (Remember the ball bouncing, using up its energy.)

More improvisation:

- Try singing any of the songs in this collection. Sing the first verse as written, and then begin to test the boundaries. Can a line in verse two take extra time? Sound to a different beat? Add notes? Subtract notes? Add a cadenza?
- Don't expect to improve the song. You can't! What you can do is explore it, feel where the spots are that invite variation (however tiny). They make the song your own.
- Listen to performances by folksingers (Jean Redpath) or song stylists (Frank Sinatra) or gospel singers (Mahalia Jackson). How do they begin the song? Where do they take it, how does it climax, and how does it end? Singers like these are your great textbooks.

Chapter 15:
Combining Ear and Eye

When we learn a song from an *Ursänger*—the original singer, one who is totally at home in the idiom—we don't have to "find" a voice: the melody is already bound together with its most characteristic sound, that of the singer who is transmitting it. Wonderful examples can be found in the Library of Congress recordings made in Southern prisons by such early jazz singers as Leadbelly, improvising on a work song with the sound of hammers in the background. (Jazz existed at first only in improvised utterance, impossible to capture on the page.) In our childhood memories, it is almost impossible to separate a song from its singer, be it a parent, neighbor, rapscallion, teacher, or concert performer. Each imbues the song with special characteristics that make the melody seem completely at home. My first memory of singer-plus-song is of my South Carolinian grandfather bouncing me on his knee to "Buffalo gals, won't you come out tonight." Touch, hearing, sight, smell, and almost taste are alive in this remembered vision.

When we meet with an unfamiliar song on the page, the challenge is to imagine the most suitable performer because the notes themselves betray none of this particularized sound. We must use all that we know of history, geography, life, love, drama, tragedy, and comedy to fit the character to the song. And there's not just one possibility. Far from it! It's almost as if the song unsung is a template, an outline, waiting to be filled with human expression. It's analogous to casting a role in a play, for the role exists first only in outline, becoming real through an individual actor. There are many possibilities, and the role itself is enriched by each new realization. The song resounds through its many soundings. The great ones can survive innumerable points of view. Some can be breathtaking, while others may be merely interesting (the critical "kiss of death" for an unsuccessful attempt).

My favorite example in this connection is the childhood favorite "Go Tell Aunt Rhody."

FIGURE 15.1. "Go Tell Aunt Rhody"

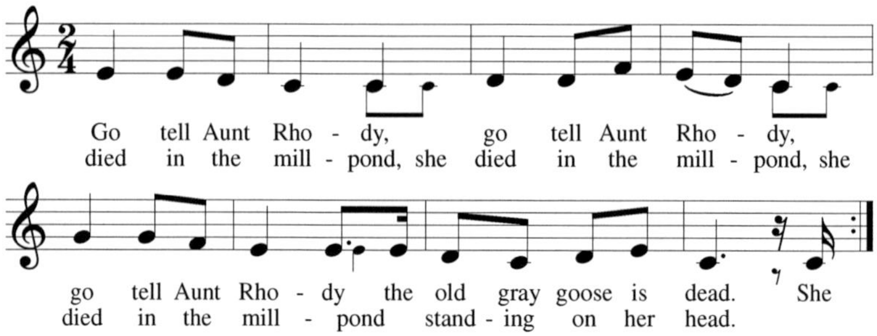

Text and tune: American folk song

It is lullaby, dance, nonsense, teasing—anything but literal. Imagine it sung by a six-year-old child jumping rope, a mother rocking her baby, or a square-dance caller. Each is totally different, though the notes on the page are the same. In fact, the notes on the page are very limited: this is not a beautiful sequence of pitches and rhythms. Simplicity is at its heart; and the tenderness of the parent-child relationship or the necessity of the dance provides an outward dress.

I learned a wonderful lesson in changed context from jazz musician Eddie Bonnemere, who proceeded to overlay my straight singing (not stopping for a moment) with the following spoken badinage:

Go tell Aunt Rhody	*Who, me?*
Go tell Aunt Rhody	*Go tell that woman?*
Go tell Aunt Rhody	*What do you want me to tell her?*
The old gray goose is dead.	*Oh, you go find someone else to run your errands.*

I sang exactly as I was used to (with some difficulty), but the innocent song was transported into the political arena of race relations by the diagonal cut of culture clash.

How are we to find the voice of a song? Imagination in sound is the prerequisite. Can you imagine just the right voice for this song? Name the singer? Is the voice male or female, trained or childlike, rich or raspy, old or young?

Try different instruments. If you heard just the right one, which is it? High or low; wind, brass, or string; recorder or oboe? Sometimes negatives are revealing—"Well, it's certainly not a trombone."

Try different settings. Are you indoors or out? Alone or with a group? In which part of the world? A specific country or region or town?

What's the human context of the scene? Are you walking, courting, storytelling, rowing a boat? Begin to see any song as an incipient opera scene. Who is singing? Where? Why? To whom? If you imagine in "living sound," you can hear how different the song is when sung by different characters in different circumstances.

The song is *never* what appears on the page, for there we find only a bunch of symbols for pitches and rhythms, measure lines, and syllables. Those are dead until they become incarnate, in every meaning of that word. On the page we have only sign-making, the signs bereft of character, of living sound. The mystery of notation is that notes written and read literally (as if the page were an end in itself) are dead, while those written under the spell of remembered or imagined sound can spring off the page.

Perhaps this is easier for us to see in terms of written words: the difference between an awkward, infelicitous sentence and one honed by imaginative craft is readily seen. The symbols used to express the idea are the same (letters and spaces), but the meaning evoked by the symbols is vastly different. Alexander Pope, in his *Essays on Criticism* (1709), expresses this paradox with typically didactic wit.

> True ease in writing comes from art, not chance,
> As those move easiest who have learn'd to dance.
> 'Tis not enough no harshness gives offence,
> The sound must seem an echo to the sense.   (363–365)

— REFLECTIONS —

Combining ear and eye:

- Begin with ear-knowledge.
    Remember a performance of a much-loved song.
    Can you write it down so that it reflects the performance?
    What kind of words do you need? What musical symbols?
- Now reverse the process. Browse through a collection of folk songs. Find ones that leap off the page, in which you can immediately hear the tone of voice of the singer.
- Find others that resist coming to life. Is it the song itself? Is it the version? Or the way it is notated? Is it your own lack of imagination?
- Recall this three-part process:
    1) The song itself as a sound experience, each time different.
    2) The notator's experience and skill in writing down a template of the tune.
    3) The reader's imagination and skill in turning symbols back into sound.

More verses to "Go Tell Aunt Rhody" (Figure 15.1—p. 152):

The one she's been saving, (3x)
To make a feather bed.

She died in the millpond, (3x)
Standing on her head.

The goslings are crying, (3x)
Because their mammy's dead.

Chapter 16:
Encountering the Page

IF WE SUBSCRIBE to the aural/oral way of teaching and learning melody advocated above, how does notation enter in? I warmly subscribe to the theories advanced in the Suzuki method of violin instruction. The principal contract is between the ear and the voice (or hand), between the hearer and the doer; the eye provides an intolerable distraction. Thus, the page should not intrude until the contract is fulfilled, e.g., the player can play or the singer can sing easily and musically. There is a very real difference between a hearer/singer and a reader/singer. In the first, the music is transmitted and received in sound waves.

Singer: Voice   *Responder*: Ear to voice (echoing sound pattern)

In the second, the visual image must be turned into imaginary sounds and then given a voice, a much more complex transaction.

Reader: Eye to brain to inner ear to voice (with no sound pattern)

When the page first enters this transaction, it should come as an aid to memory. It serves as the visual image of a song already well loved. It is someone's attempt to turn those sounds into a readable graph. For young children, it might come as the first songbook introduced in a school where every song is lovingly taught by ear before it is found in the book. Never is the child asked to read an unfamiliar song; the page is used as backup.

There are all kinds of pre-page games to play that foster a beginning understanding of pitch and rhythm. Draw the curves of the melody in the air as you sing. Count while another voice sings. Sing syllables (I much prefer movable *do*). Conduct as you sing. Dance as you sing. Clap the song rhythms while you tap your foot to the beat. The more the singer gets the notion that the song is moving through space (up and down for pitches) and time (beat and duration for rhythms), the easier the transfer to the page will be.

When children are a bit older, they might be presented with a piece of manuscript paper with one-half of a familiar song written on it in the teacher's hand, with an invitation to finish it. No helps are barred. The child can consult or copy or try to figure it out on his or her own. Then problems are discussed together, the best version agreed on, and another song assigned. I'm old-fashioned enough to prefer that this be done by hand rather than on the computer. This is part of learning to draw, to form letters, to enjoy calligraphy. There is a direct communication between the hand and the page that is lacking with the computer.

An interesting point here is that breathing is automatic for the hearer-singer. One simply imitates the example as well as possible, and while different breath patterns may emerge, they do so without conscious volition. The moment the song is notated, those breaths disappear. The simplest way to notate a melody does not include rests for breathing. Rather, one makes the easy assumption that the singer will continue breathing! But as notation copes with more detail, it demands more and more precision, and the page becomes more and more complex.

When I taught piano to eight-year-olds, the only book we used for three months was a small manuscript book in which either they or I wrote whatever was needed. We began with lots of keyboard exploration: find the F-sharps with your eyes closed; play any note and then a half step or whole step up and down; five-finger short songs in all keys, etc. Then, I taught by rote one song per week (expressive playing came first: fingering a phrase for *legato*, lifting the hand off the keyboard for each breath). We would then write it down together. I included some basic harmony as their fingers were able to play chords (were they ever eager to!), and by Christmas they could play several familiar carols in duet with me, either the melody or the accompaniment, in several keys. Then I gave them their first piano book, the first time they'd seen big engraved notes, and told them to go as far as they could by the next lesson. This kid stuff was so easy, they would finish three or four books before they got to their own level. The point: they were never first asked to read, only to sing and play, then write. The reading came as an inevitable result.

I had another experience with a high school guitar player who was applying to a conservatory for advanced study. They asked for notation of his original songs, and he had no idea how to write them down. A friend brought us together, and it took me three lessons to give him all the information he needed. The first session was rhythm. I had him watch his foot as he played (he was good!) to find out the beat and meter of his song. Then we ruled off several blank measures on manuscript paper and put checks above the staff to indicate the foot taps. Listening to his own melody, he discovered long and short notes. The symbols for these were easily demonstrated, and he began to learn to count internally as he figured out the durations.

The next session was about pitch. We started with the strings of the guitar, representing them on staff paper (he was fascinated). All he had to do was look where his finger was on the string and transfer it to the page. Because we'd already graphed the rhythm, the tune came out right the first time. The third lesson, of course, was chord theory, and he knew a lot of that already. I told him to come back if he needed more. I never saw him again. That's knowing the music first and then adding the page.

A totally different experience happens to me as a composer. I don't even remember learning to read music—it happened early and easily. As I began to write, I think I was caught in the old bind of writing something simple and then playing it the way it looked: square. But as I learned to be a better listener (through the work with Shaw), I got more and more frustrated with the page. It can't transmit the music—only the most raw pitch and rhythm, with hints for articulation. And when I look later at a page of my own music, I don't really *see* it at all—I *hear* the sounds it reminds me of and play/sing those. Needless to say, I'm my own worst proofreader.

The very act of notation changes the aural experience. As long as the song is sound, it's free. When you write it down, it's like killing the butterfly. You have reduced the song to a set of component parts that no longer work. One can teach people to read exactly what's on the page and end up with un-music. All life is gone from it. This kind of reading actually rewards unmusicality, the musical sin of dullness. If a reader is not in tune with the style of the song, she cannot bring it to life again. I once (never again) adjudicated at a high school festival where four choruses in sequence sang the same choral work to a group of judges scattered around a darkened auditorium. We were to judge only on the basis of fidelity to the page with no consideration for expressivity or style, no deviation from square pitch and rhythm. The groups that won sounded lifeless and dull, and the one choir that brought vitality and enjoyment to the singing was shot down by everyone except me.

The only fruitful relationship to the page is a love-hate one. We should be very clear about what the page can and can't transmit. Written notes and rhythms are not music, but deplorably inadequate indications of a physical reality. Think of the relation of the recipe to the food. If the ingredients are stale or spoiled, one can follow the recipe exactly and end up with an inedible dish. If the musical materials are uninflected or carelessly presented, we make sounds that no one wants to listen to. We don't eat the page of the cookbook, and we don't sing the writing in the songbook.

Notation can give us a working suggestion of what that reality might be. That's all that our printed music is. Whenever I hear a composer say, "Play it just the way it is on the page," I wonder at the basic lack of understanding. Are they like the composers who are satisfied with the sounds that come out of a computer? I myself prefer the living voice.

— REFLECTIONS —

Encountering the page:

- Because the page cannot possibly represent the sound in all its aspects, the person making the symbols on the page had to make many decisions. Does he or she choose the simplest possible notation, trusting the reader to interpret?
- Should every possible nuance be marked? Should the reader be told whether to take the marking literally or with some freedom (e.g., swing, freely, *espressivo*)?
- Here is the first phrase of a familiar spiritual. Which version do you prefer? Why?

FIGURE 16.1. "Swing Low, Sweet Chariot"—basic

Swing low, sweet cha - ri - ot,—— com - in' for to car - ry me home;

FIGURE 16.2. "Swing Low, Sweet Chariot"—pop style

Swing low, sweet cha - ri - ot,—— com - in' for to car - ry me home;

FIGURE 16.3. "Swing Low, Sweet Chariot"—swung

Swing low, sweet cha - ri - ot,—— com - in' for to car - ry me home;

FIGURE 16.4. "Swing Low, Sweet Chariot"—improvised variation

And here is "Oh, Shenandoah" notated to try to account for the many crosscurrents contained in the flow. I imagined trying to show an instrumentalist how much expressivity comes through the text, including the small dynamic changes within a long *crescendo*. But for all practical purposes, it's disastrously overmarked.

FIGURE 16.5. "Oh, Shenandoah" (see Figure 1.1)

NOTATION: THE BAR SINISTER

CHAPTER 17:
THE PAGE ITSELF

I'VE OFTEN LONGED for a creative calligrapher—or maybe a sophisticated cartoonist—to make some adjustments to our current system of notation. Wouldn't it be nice to have noteheads of varying sizes to indicate accents?

FIGURE 17.1. Varying notehead sizes

Or noteheads of varying shapes for different words?

FIGURE 17.2. Varying notehead shapes

Couldn't the stems lean forward for an *accelerando* or back for *ritardando*?

FIGURE 17.3. Leaning stems

Or how about chant melodies in free rhythm? Wouldn't it be better to abandon the standard notehead with its inner message of sameness, of counting, of metrical exactitude? How about a variant on the old chant notation, using only a black and a white notehead of different sizes and at least two different phrase endings?

FIGURE 17.4. Variant notation for "By'm Bye" (see Figure 3.3)

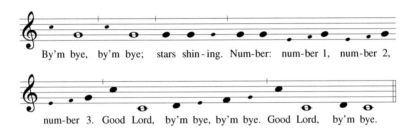

By'm bye, by'm bye; stars shin-ing. Num-ber: num-ber 1, num-ber 2,

num-ber 3. Good Lord, by'm bye, by'm bye. Good Lord, by'm bye.

I'd love to hold music written on elastic paper that could stretch to accommodate a *rubato*. Could we change color when the tempo changes? (It's amazing how many people will simply not notice a "Twice as fast" marking.) Could we revive the Gregorian courtesy of indicating at the end of a staff the first pitch on the next line? First and second endings are a constant snare. There must be a better way.

Here's another picture: imagine someone translating a song into needlepoint. There is a loosely woven canvas upon which the stitches are placed. (Think vertical strands for pitch, horizontal for rhythm.) It would be quite easy to place "Twinkle, Twinkle Little Star" at the intersection of each pitch and duration strand. But what about spirituals? Or jazz? These are notated with the same devices as classical music, but in practice both pitches and durations are bent: there are blue notes and a constant teasing of the beat. Both pitches and rhythms would wander from the intersection. A song written by George Gershwin uses the same symbols as "Twinkle," but to vastly different affect. Because we have this style in our ears, we would never sing it exactly as written. The scale tones and beat are there, but the performer is literally playing with both, and wonderful performers are distinguished precisely by their success at this game. I love to ponder the question: what is Ella Fitzgerald's responsibility to the page?

—ELLA AND GEORGE—

What is Ella Fitzgerald's responsibility to a page of Gershwin? Let's assume that she first heard the song in someone else's interpretation. She might at first imitate that or adapt it, or even go back and see what he actually wrote. But there is NO responsibility to sing exactly what is on the page. Why? Because this is a living language—the idiom is spoken now—so that-which-cannot-be-notated is intuitively supplied. The beat will swing, the words are to be played with, the specific rhythms may be widely varied. In fact, she will never sing it as written: the only person who might so interpret the page is an unskilled piano player.

She will never even begin with the expectation of doing it exactly as printed. That's not the aim. (Is it for Mozart?) She will make it hers, faithful to the template of the song, but moving way beyond it. What is the template? It's the beat (tempo plus quality of beat), and the curve of the line—perhaps starting with the written pitches, never the mathematical rhythms—with expected variations. (Mozart, too?) Her voice and her style are built into her rendition: the performance will be a fusion of Gershwin and Fitzgerald. (Also Mozart?) The variations she plays on the original are her own. Other aspiring performers will copy her style, but until they make their own fusion, their performances will be dull, while she's incapable of doing it wrong. She's always ready to begin the game at the beginning, creating the song anew.

(Instrumentally speaking, things are different. One must master the technique before one can play the concerto. But I still don't think that technique should be learned unmusically. If scales and exercises are never allowed to be played mechanically, the musical aspects can dominate and energize the player and listener.)

And how about George? I'm sure he doesn't want to hear his song mauled by an inexperienced hand, but I'm equally sure that he doesn't want to hear it correct to the page but dull. I can't answer for him, but I suspect that he would cherish the times that Ella took his basic material and transformed it. (Mozart, too?)

In other words, our culture's deification of the page produces some strange results. When slavish accuracy is taught and valued over musicality, something is wrong. The eye has triumphed over the ear, and the promise of the sound cannot be fulfilled.

— REFLECTIONS —

The page itself:

- Look at the score of a popular song you know by ear.

    Does it look like it sounds?

    Does it sound like it looks?

    Can you perform it exactly (metronomically) as written?

    Is it in the right key for your voice?

    Where do you breathe? Is it notated?

    What do you need to add to the page (or change) in order to sing it?

    Does it sound like what you know in your ear? Why? Why not?

- What is the difference between music we know because we live in its culture and music from a past age or different culture? How does that affect what we see on the page?

- How can we overcome that gulf? Can we do it without ever hearing an idiomatic performance? What is an "acceptable" attempt? What is not acceptable? (Remember that dullness is the cardinal sin.)

- What is the difference between a page of Mozart and a page of Gershwin? Can you verbalize that-which-cannot-be-notated?

FIGURE 17.5. Wolfgang Amadeus Mozart's *La Clemenza de Tito*, 1791

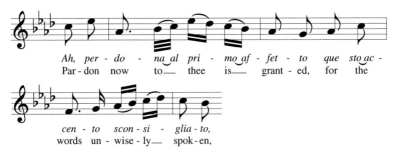

FIGURE 17.6. "Someone to Watch Over Me"

Music and Lyrics by George Gershwin and Ira Gershwin copyright © 1926, WB Music Corp. (Renewed) This arrangement copyright © WB Music Corp. All Rights Reserved.

CHAPTER 18:
ONE COMPOSER'S RELATIONSHIP WITH THE PAGE

When I compose, I don't approach either the page or the piano until the sound of the piece is quite clear in my head. It's not finished by any means, but I do know the tempo and sonority, the shape of the whole, and various themes and ideas. It's a vision. (I wish there were an aural-equivalent word.) I don't begin to write until it's like taking dictation—the idea is clear, and I'm listening to a performance as I write. As I fill in the sketch, the performance becomes more and more complete, and as I add the final touches to the page, the same transformation is going on in my head. This is an ideal performance: no mistakes, no page turns, no uncertainties. But it isn't yet sound—not until I hear the work performed does my vision come to life.

Inevitably, there is a gulf between what I see and hear on my page and what another person perceives. If I'm conducting, I can quickly demonstrate to the performers what I want and let them mark their pages to remind themselves. But if I'm not present, there's no way for me to insure a sympathetic performance. I'm often astonished at the lack of common sense in many performers' note reading. Where I would accent an obvious syllable, or turn a phrase suddenly tender, or keep up a dance tempo, others will solemnly plod through with no expression. They're reading the notes instead of the words. When I hear this, I add to the page some kind of mark, an accent, or "tenderly," or "*non ritardando*." I dislike overmarking because it makes the page a confusion—but it's also my responsibility to give as clear an indication as possible of how I want the notes and rhythms to sound.

It seems to me that there are three parts to the composing and notating of music. First comes establishing a tempo and sonority for the as yet unformed idea. I must sense first the relative speed and dance qualities of the music. Then comes the kind of sound: vocal or instrumental, rich or light, high or low, until I've found a place for this piece in the universe where time intersects with sound. This is usually given to me by the text, which also dictates the form of the work. Thus, long before I start writing, I know the approximate length of the piece, its tempo, meter, and key. As this is taking shape in my head, I'm acutely conscious of the mood these phrases evoke. If I can name it or be specific about it, it will help to focus all the notes and rhythms that follow.

Second, I listen in my head to the voices singing (or violins playing) the specific notes, the melodies, the extensions between verses, and the changing colors that reflect in the music what the words imply.

Third is writing down what I've heard, and this is usually easy. I'm suspicious if I have to pick up an eraser. It means the ideas haven't gestated enough. All those decisions about how to get from here to there should have been made in my imagination, not on the page.

Last, I must look at the page as if with new eyes, seeing what other markings will help the reader/performer sense what I have heard. Somehow this is always hard for me. (I love my Bach keyboard volumes where there is no editing: I can decide for myself about tempo and phrasing and change my mind as often as I like.) I do check the score at the piano before I send it off and make any adjustments that seem advisable. I never like to submit a piece for publication until I've had a chance to hear it in performance. It doesn't feel finished until a year or so later, when it's had a chance to "season," when I can hear it a bit objectively and add any additional markings.

For the reader/performer, the notes and rhythms are the first things that catch the eye. But if there is no recognition that they come out of a deep context, they are liable to be misunderstood. In vocal music, I recommend beginning with the text and sensing its mood, its rhythms, and its voice before integrating it with the notes. In a peculiar, backwards way, the other markings should be presumed to apply specifically to the text and applied there before the phrases are sung or played.

Quiet, flowing

Teach me to feel another's woe,	*mp*
To hide the fault I see;	
That mercy I to others show,	*espressivo*
That mercy show to me.	

Notice first the tempo and mood markings. The only way the composer can indicate these is with some words (and/or a metronome marking) at the beginning of the piece. They color everything that follows: always read the text within those parameters (i.e., free or metered, lilting or admonitory, etc.). What is the dance? Realize that tempo is always relative to the occasion, the performers, the hall, and the energy. So what are the outside limits? Notice fermatas and any changes of tempo. Find a voice and sonority that grow out of this text at this tempo in this mood (e.g., formal/colloquial, young/old, serious/playful, literal/ironic).

If I am right, thy grace impart	*mp*
Still in the right to stay;	
If I am wrong, oh teach my heart	*mf pleading*
To find that better way.	

Mean though I am, not wholly so   *mp*
Since quicken'd by thy breath:
Oh lead me wheresoe'er I go   *mf espressivo*
Through this day's life or death.
               —Alexander Pope

Now read this text in the rhythms notated on the page, without losing any of the foregoing subtleties (Figure 18.1). Add all the dynamic markings and the articulation symbols: accents, slurs, rests, minute changes in approach (e.g., *legato/non legato, marcato/staccato,* etc.).

When the text sounds as if it is being read by a wonderful actor, you are ready to add the pitches. They should slip into place almost effortlessly, carried along by the energies already moving in the room.

Keep singing; don't stop at verse endings. Try to capture the flow of the whole piece. *Now,* finally, you can rehearse the notes and rhythms for accuracy because you know what they mean. You are riding on the current sensed by the creator, and all these components fit together in an organic whole. This is truly to read music.

Do you remember that vision in the composer's head? You are on your way to realizing it. But the final paradox is that the sound can't ever completely fulfill the vision, precisely because the vision was only imagined. The performance is in real sound waves and can be real *music* only if those reading the page are aware of all the subtleties. Each performance is going to be different because there's no possibility of an exact repetition. Ah, that's the mystery of incarnation, the mystery of music and theatre and religion, which demand for their realization the genius and exasperation of human beings, with all their promise and fallibility. That's why we must keep performing again and again. Next time we might get even closer to that illusive/elusive ideal.

FIGURE 18.1. Variant on WALLINGFORD

Text: Alexander Pope
Tune: Connecticut, 19th c., arr. Alice Parker © 2000 Lawson Gould,
Parker: And Sing Eternally

— REFLECTIONS —

One composer's relationship with the page—
Folk songs and composed music:

- Folk songs and hymns are usually written without any performance markings. When you decide how you want to sing a particular song, try to add some symbols, both for your own clarity and so that another person can get a sense of your vision.

- Mark a song the way you sing it, later handing the paper to another. Does his or her singing sound like what you intended? Listen for what transmits and what does not. Now try to adjust the markings (without speaking or singing) to get the performance you envision. Now try to do all this by singing with the other imitating. Which works better? Why?

- Composed music usually has helpful markings. The historical precedent was to use none when everyone was part of the same culture (as in gospel music today—people *know* the style). But as the composer became more and more separated from the performance by space and time, markings became necessary. Throughout the nineteenth century, they proliferated until there were composers who marked almost every note.

- What page can you trust?
  1) If it is a composer you know and admire, trust the page. Obey all the markings: bend your interpretation to fit them. If there are no markings, experiment with the style.
  2) If you do not know the composer, make a real effort to learn the page as written. If the symbols make no sense to you, decide if the piece is worth learning. If it is, remark it.
  3) If the song is from a source with no markings, find a way to sing it that communicates to you and others. Then add your markings.

- Always ask the page: Who put these symbols here? The composer? An editor? An arranger? Can you trust them? How many layers of editing are there between the composer or first singer and the page you are holding? Look at the composer's original if you can. Remember, your job is to bring the template to life.

Articulation and other performance markings:

- Ask the page:

  Who put these marks on this page?

  Who sang this song first?

  How many steps are there between that version and this?

  In what language was the original?

    Which version? (How spelled, pronounced?)

    Is it a translation or adaptation, or completely new?

- Ask the song:

  Who are you: pitch or rhythm?

  Where do you breathe? How?

  What mode or scale are you in? True? Altered? Partial? Name?

  What meter? Simple? Complex? Clearly notated?

  What is your dance? How might I move to you?

  What is your tempo?

  What is your sonority? Vocal? Instrumental?

  What is your structure? Repetitions?

  What is your function? In life cycle? In work/play?

  Who sang you first? When, where, why, and how?

    Trace different versions in history or geography.

  What mood do you establish?

  Who is singing you now, in my imagination?

Rule 1: Read the text first, finding a "voice" for it.

 Note spoken rhythms, accents, and dynamics.

 Note loaded syllables and throwaway sounds.

Rule 2: In singing, no two adjacent notes are ever the same volume or energy.

 You are either going somewhere or coming back.

 You are either increasing tension or resolving it.

COMMUNICATING THE SONG

Chapter 19:
One Conductor's Relationship with Song

Many years of songleading have confirmed my feeling that conducting as it is usually taught is an adjunct of the page and of instrumental music. It is an interpretation of the page for performers who lead those who must learn to divide their attention between the page and the stick. (In most conservatories, conducting applies only to orchestras: choral conducting needs the qualifier.) The conductor is always concerned with the score: learning to read, interpret, mark, and provide appropriate gestures for its performance. The players are also bound to the page. They need to learn to read those gestures and respond to them at the same time that they read and play the page. They depend on the gestures to focus the ensemble and keep it together. Woe betide them if something disturbs this double focus.

Quite different is the experience of the songleader, working in the realm of the ear; here the ear must dominate. The first requirement is that the singers learn to listen to one another. Singing loudly without listening leads to the football cheer syndrome: energetic but not particularly musical. When someone says, "Just sing out! The sound doesn't matter," I think, "Poor music! All it *is* is sound."

The leader's challenge is to embody the song, to capture its essence in voice, face, body, and gesture. There is no page to get in the way, to distract the auditor's attention. This is the language of the kindergarten classroom, of the nighttime campfire circle, of the jazz player and blues singer, of the church congregation.

Song leading is an ancient profession. Watch how similar are enliveners of song from different countries. Leaders and singers are completely caught up in the experience of capturing a song, and niceties of correct gesture or language are completely irrelevant. The international gestures trace the curves of phrase, swoop up and down to high pitches and low, shrink in size for quiet, explode for accent—march, dance, cradle, attack—a talented mime is at work. The trick is to anticipate what the singers need in energy or beat or accent or mood.

Yes, the notes and rhythms are being taught, but only as part of a whole, which is principally communicative. So those other markings assume priority. The values most desired in performance are taught first: listening, ensemble, style, tuning, and rhythmic vitality. Never can it be dull. The leader establishes pitch and rhythm by lining out the phrase and then listens to see if the group is catching on to his or her vision. If the response is insufficient, the leader models again, even more demonstratively, again listening for the quality of the answer. We don't progress further until the singers have realized that they must listen and allow their voices to join the sound of the whole group.

Rote teaching demands lots of repetition, but this is not boring if the leader keeps asking for more and more expressive sound. A completely untutored listener or singer can immediately hear the difference between musical and unmusical performance and is unreasonably delighted with progress. The mood, once established, is maintained until it comes to flower in beautiful performance. It is not difficult to achieve this when the whole focus is on the single line: part-singing and harmonies pose different challenges. But I often tell my students that getting the melody just right is 100 percent: anything after that is gravy. After all, the melody is what you want people to remember after the singing. If it's well taught, it is cradled in the singers' inmost memory.

— REFLECTIONS —

One conductor's relationship with song:

My thought on completing these pages is one of astonishment that I have found so much to say about single lines of melody. There are so many ways to examine any tune, and so many ways to perform it. We should value lasting songs as unique manifestations of human discourse and sing them with respect and imagination as well as love.

Another volume will look at the response to melody: the phrases that may develop out of a song in an answering voice. We will find that this discloses new truths about the song and provides a first step for beginning composers and arrangers to learn their craft. Like this book, it attempts to deal with what we don't dare discuss in most of our music-making and teaching: those mysterious elements that touch our ears, minds, hearts, and spirits, those subtle movements of sound waves that can be heard but are beyond notation or verbal analysis. It will provide a framework for the science of harmony and an introduction to counterpoint that makes it a natural response for all singers.

But even now you should be much more aware of the many strands that go into a melody and the myriad ways that it may be sung. Don't hesitate to enter into the circle of those who communicate easily through song and find infinite joy and solace in so doing.

—A Walk in the Woods—

(as told to me many years ago)

An old teacher and a young student are walking on a sunny afternoon, unhurried, in companionable silence. Their path leads them into a leafy wood, winding on into a small clearing that is warm in the sunlight. The teacher walks ahead into the center of the meadow and slowly raises his arms. Everything begins to sing: the sunlight, the leaves, the plants and small flowers, the grasses, the breeze. All the songs overlap and interweave, endless, subtle, sweet. They continue as long as the teacher stands still: when his arms fall, the sounds die away. The student, spellbound at the edge of the clearing, approaches the teacher. "How do you do that?" he asks in wonder. "It's very simple," is the quiet reply. "They're doing it all the time. You just have to know how to bring it out."

Chapter 20:
The Circle of Song

The circle begins
when a song is sung—
newly created or recreated.

- Folk song:
    A singer makes up a song, singing it into being.

    A listener hears, joins in, imitates, adapts, passes it along.

    Other individuals or groups join the circle.

    The melody changes, remaining true to itself, yet yielding to variant patterns.

    There is no one true version: the one you knew first is probably best for you.

    The nature of the song is constant, subtle variation.

- Composed or written song:
    A composer makes up a song, writing it into being.

    A reader takes up the page, transposing it back into mental sound.

    The performer moves the mental image into physical sound.

    A listener hears the song and joins the circle.

The circle is complete
when the creator, performer, and listener
are made one through the song.

The circle is interrupted
when one or more of the links
is imperfect.

- Limitations:
  Composers, readers, and performers are limited by their own
  imagination, craft, and experience.
  The page imposes its own limitations:
  If the notation is oversimplified or overcomplicated.
  If the language has been tampered with.
  If changes have been made by an insensitive or unmusical
  person.

Can you complete the circle each time you sing?

BIBLIOGRAPHY

Buchanan, Annabel Morris. *Folk Hymns of America*. New York: J. Fischer & Bro., 1938.

Carse, James P. *Finite and Infinite Games*. New York: Free Press, 1986.

———. *The Silence of God: Meditations on Prayer*. New York: Macmillan, 1985.

"The Chickens They Are Crowing." *English Folksongs from the Southern Appalachians*. Collected by Cecil J. Sharp. Edited by Maud Karpeles. Oxford: Oxford University Press, 1932.

Colvin, Tom, tr. CHEREPONI. Ghanaian folk song. Carol Stream, IL: Hope Publishing Company, 1969.

Dickinson, Emily. "Exultation Is the Going," *Complete Poems #76*. Edited by Johnson. Boston: Little Brown, 1960.

"Domine sancte." *Liber Usualis*. Tournai, Belgium: Desclee & Co., 1952, xxxvi.

Dudley-Smith, Timothy. HYFRYDOL. Text to first verse. Carol Stream, IL: Hope Publishing, 1984.

Feliciano, Francisco F. "Wasdin." *Hymns from the Four Winds*. Nashville: Abingdon Press, 1983.

Funk, Joseph. A Compilation of Genuine Church Music. 2nd ed. Winchester, VA: New Salem, 1835.

Gershwin, George, and Ira Gershwin. "I Got Rhythm." Miami, FL: Warner Brothers Publications, Inc., 1930.

———. "Someone to Watch Over Me." Miami, FL: Warner Brothers Publications, Inc., 1926.

Havelock, Eric. *The Muse Learns to Write: Reflections on Orality and Literacy from Antiquity to the Present*. New Haven: Yale University Press, 1986.

Hibbard, E., tr. IMAYO from *Cantate Domino: An Ecumenical Hymn Book*. 12th c. Japanese. Japanese Hymnal Committee, 1962.

"Kinga Tune." Traditional Tanzanian tune with Swahili text edited by Howard S. Olson. 1977.

"Kyrie" from *Missa Orbis factor*. *Liber Usualis*. Solesmes, France: S.A. La Froidfontaine, 1997, 46.

Lomax, John A., and Alan Lomax. "Dink's Song." *American Ballads and Folk Songs*. New York: Macmillan, 1934, 193–195.

Mozart, Wolfgang Amadeus. *La Clemenza de Tito*, 1791.

Parker, Alice. "My Uncle Daniel." *The Ponder Heart*. Musical score, 1982.

———. Variant on WALLINGFORD. *Parker: And Sing Eternally*. New York: Lawson Gould, 2000.

Pritchard, Rowland Hugh. HYFRYDOL.

Sandburg, Carl, comp. *The American Songbag.* New York: Harcourt, Brace, 1927.

Sayers, Dorothy L. *The Whimsical Christian: Christian Letters to a Post-Christian World.* New York: Collier Books, 1978.

Schumann, Robert. *Nachtstück*, Op. 23, No. 4.

Stravinsky, Igor, and Robert Craft. *Dialogues and a Diary.* Garden City, NY: Doubleday, 1963.

Vaughan Williams, Ralph. "For All the Saints." *The English Hymnal.* London: Oxford University Press, 1906.

Welty, Eudora. "My Uncle Daniel." *The Ponder Heart.* 1953, 1954.

About the Author

COMPOSER, CONDUCTOR AND TEACHER **Alice Parker** was born in Boston in 1925. She began composing early and wrote her first orchestral score while still in high school. Parker graduated from Smith College with a major in music performance and composition and then received her master's degree from the Juilliard School, where she studied choral conducting with Robert Shaw.

Her lifework has been in choral and vocal music, combining composing, conducting, and teaching in a creative balance. Her arrangements with Robert Shaw of folk songs, hymns, and spirituals form an enduring repertoire for choruses all around the world. She continues composing in many forms, from operas to cantatas, sacred anthems to secular dances, song cycles to string quartets. She has been commissioned by such groups as the Vancouver Chamber Chorus, the Atlanta Symphony Chorus, and Chanticleer. Her many conducting and teaching engagements keep her traveling around the United States and Canada.

In 1985, she founded Melodious Accord, Inc., a nonprofit group that presents choral concerts and sponsors workshops, symposia, and her many professional appearances. The Fellows programs have provided unique training for composers, conductors, and song leaders. She has made eleven acclaimed recordings with the Musicians of Melodious Accord, a sixteen-voice professional chorus. The group has received generous support from the National Endowment for the Arts, the Copland Foundation, and the New York State Council for the Arts.

Alice Parker serves on the board of Chorus America and was honored by them and the American Guild of Organists and the Hymn Society in her seventy-fifth year. Her techniques have encouraged a generation of music teachers and choral conductors to think about music and the act of conducting in new ways. No less an authority than Robert Shaw himself has said of Parker that "she possesses a rare and creative musical intelligence."

Now a resident of western Massachusetts, Parker has published books on melodic styles, choral improvisation, and "Good Singing in Church." Five videos show her work with hymns and folk songs. She is the recipient of four honorary doctorates and the Smith College Medal. For more about Alice Parker, see www.aliceparker.com.